BUSINESS ISSUES, COMPETITION AND ENTREPRENEURSHIP

THE CONSTRUCTION SECTOR IN THE U.S. ECONOMY: ELEMENTS AND EMPLOYMENT ANALYSES

BUSINESS ISSUES, COMPETITION AND ENTREPRENEURSHIP

Additional books in this series can be found on Nova's website under the Series tab.

Additional E-books in this series can be found on Nova's website under the E-book tab.

ECONOMIC ISSUES, PROBLEMS AND PERSPECTIVES

Additional books in this series can be found on Nova's website under the Series tab.

Additional E-books in this series can be found on Nova's website under the E-book tab.

BUSINESS ISSUES, COMPETITION AND ENTREPRENEURSHIP

THE CONSTRUCTION SECTOR IN THE U.S. ECONOMY: ELEMENTS AND EMPLOYMENT ANALYSES

NELSON M. MCDONALD
AND
CLAUDE A. MARSHALL
EDITORS

Nova Science Publishers, Inc.
New York

Library of Congress Cataloging-in-Publication Data

ISBN 978-1-61942-893-5

Published by Nova Science Publishers, Inc. †New York

CONTENTS

PREFACE

The construction sector is a major component of the U.S. economy. During the past decade, construction was a prime beneficiary of low interest rates and the housing-led economic boom, but was also one of the largest casualties of the subsequent financial crisis. There are three major segments of the construction sector: residential, commercial, and industrial/heavy construction. The segments have unique market characteristics and are subject to cyclical economic forces, though in somewhat differing ways. This book outlines the structure of the construction industry and describes congressional initiatives that affect the sector.

Chapter 1 - The construction sector is a major component of the U.S. economy. During the past decade, construction was a prime beneficiary of low interest rates and the housing-led economic boom, but was also one of the largest casualties of the subsequent financial crisis. Construction spending comprised about 7%-8% of U.S. annual economic output from 1995 to mid-2000, reaching nearly 9% of gross domestic product at the peak of the housing run-up in 2006, before declining to about 5% in 2010. Likewise, construction employment ranged from a low of about 4.6 million during the early 1990s to a high of 7.7 million during the 2006 housing boom, and was about 5.5 million in early 2011.

There are three major segments of the construction sector: residential, commercial, and industrial/heavy construction. The segments have unique market characteristics and are subject to cyclical economic forces, though in somewhat differing ways. Commercial and residential construction have been hard hit by the severe contraction in private-sector financing and building activity that began in 2006. While public works spending has been steadier, it may come under pressure as state and local governments pare outlays to reduce budget deficits.

Public spending has accounted for an increasing share of U.S. construction activity since 2007, due to the slowdown in private-sector construction as well as a substantial increase in government infrastructure aid. Government-funded projects made up about 40% of U.S. construction activity in 2010, compared to about 20% in 2006. While state and local governments provided the bulk of these dollars, federal construction spending has risen to a record, due in part to the 2009 economic stimulus legislation, the American Recovery and Reinvestment Act (ARRA; P.L. 111- 5). Faced with a downbeat outlook, and with stimulus funding winding down, representatives of the various construction segments have asked the 112th Congress to approve additional initiatives to bolster the industry, including an infrastructure bank to finance long-term projects and financial incentives to make commercial buildings more energy-efficient.

Chapter 2 - Construction occupations accounted for 4.9 million jobs in May 2010, down from 6.5 million in May 2006 when employment in construction-related occupations reached a peak. Since then, employment has declined among establishments whose primary output was construction or construction trade services and among workers performing construction-related activities in any industry. Employment in 40 of the 46 construction occupations decreased over this time, with some occupations declining by half. The employment declines were more extreme in some industries than others. Employment declines were often steeper among the lower-paid construction helper occupations.

This visual essay examines employment and wages of workers in construction occupations in May 2010, when construction employment was at its lowest point in over a decade. Some comparisons are made with employment and earnings in May 2006.

Chapter 3 - Construction employment fell by 1.5 million[1] during the December 2007–June 2009 recession,[2] bringing employment in the industry to the lowest level since March 1998. The losses during the recession represented a 19.8-percent decline in construction employment, the largest percent decline of any nonfarm industry supersector. The majority of the losses came during the last 9 months of the recession, when employment declined by 1 million. Job losses averaged 49,000 per month between December 2007 and September 2008 and then accelerated to an average of 115,000 per month through June 2009. Those construction firms which engaged primarily in residential construction activities started losing jobs more than a year before the recession started, and those firms which conducted primarily nonresidential and heavy construction projects did not start losing jobs until the onset of recession.

Chapter 4 - Employment Projections Program data are used to estimate employment impacts due to the recent housing market cycle, and alternative "nonbubble" demand scenarios indicate that at the peak of the bubble, in 2005, approximately 1.2 million to 1.7 million residential-construction-related jobs were attributable to "bubble-related demand."

Chapter 5 - Beginning around 2001, employment in residential construction rose much faster than that in nonresidential construction, but the former then began a precipitous drop earlier than the latter; in addition, employee compensation has grown faster in recent years in nonresidential building construction than in residential building construction.

In: The Construction Sector in the U.S. Economy ISBN 978-1-61942-893-5
Editors: N. M. McDonald et al.

Chapter 1

THE CONSTRUCTION SECTOR IN THE U.S. ECONOMY*

Suzanne M. Kirchhoff

SUMMARY

The construction sector is a major component of the U.S. economy. During the past decade, construction was a prime beneficiary of low interest rates and the housing-led economic boom, but was also one of the largest casualties of the subsequent financial crisis. Construction spending comprised about 7%-8% of U.S. annual economic output from 1995 to mid-2000, reaching nearly 9% of gross domestic product at the peak of the housing run-up in 2006, before declining to about 5% in 2010. Likewise, construction employment ranged from a low of about 4.6 million during the early 1990s to a high of 7.7 million during the 2006 housing boom, and was about 5.5 million in early 2011.

There are three major segments of the construction sector: residential, commercial, and industrial/heavy construction. The segments have unique market characteristics and are subject to cyclical economic forces, though in somewhat differing ways. Commercial and residential construction have been hard hit by the severe contraction in private-sector financing and building

* This is an edited, reformatted and augmented version of the Congressional Research Service Report for Congress R41806 dated May 3, 2011.

activity that began in 2006. While public works spending has been steadier, it may come under pressure as state and local governments pare outlays to reduce budget deficits.

Public spending has accounted for an increasing share of U.S. construction activity since 2007, due to the slowdown in private-sector construction as well as a substantial increase in government infrastructure aid. Government-funded projects made up about 40% of U.S. construction activity in 2010, compared to about 20% in 2006. While state and local governments provided the bulk of these dollars, federal construction spending has risen to a record, due in part to the 2009 economic stimulus legislation, the American Recovery and Reinvestment Act (ARRA; P.L. 111- 5). Faced with a downbeat outlook, and with stimulus funding winding down, representatives of the various construction segments have asked the 112th Congress to approve additional initiatives to bolster the industry, including an infrastructure bank to finance long-term projects and financial incentives to make commercial buildings more energy-efficient.

INTRODUCTION

The construction sector is a major component of the U.S. economy. During the past decade, construction was a prime beneficiary of low interest rates and the housing-led economic boom, but was also one of the largest casualties of the subsequent financial crisis. Construction spending comprised about 7%-8% of U.S. annual economic output from 1995 to mid-2000, reaching a perhaps unsustainable peak of nearly 9% of gross domestic product during the housing run-up in 2006, before declining to about 5% in 2010. Likewise, construction employment ranged from about 4.6 million during the 1991 recession to a high of 7.7 million in 2006, and fell to about 5.5 million in early 2011.[1]

There are three major segments of the construction sector: residential, commercial, and industrial/heavy construction. The segments have unique market characteristics and are subject to cyclical economic forces, though in somewhat differing ways. Commercial and residential construction have been hard hit by the severe contraction in private-sector financing and building activity since 2006. Public works spending has been steadier, and has accounted for an increasing share of U.S. construction activity since 2007. Government-funded projects made up about 40% of U.S. construction activity in 2010, compared to about 20% in 2006.[2] While state and local governments provided the bulk of these dollars, federal construction spending has risen to a record, due in part to the 2009 economic stimulus legislation, the American Recovery and Reinvestment Act (ARRA; P.L. 111-5).[3]

Measured in Billions of Chained 2005 Dollars

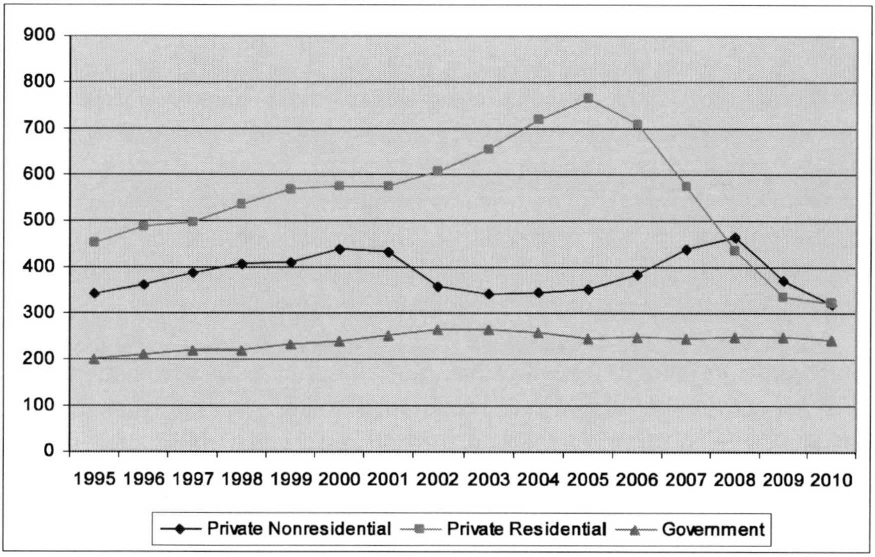

Source: Bureau of Economic Analysis.

Figure 1. U.S. Construction Investment.

In addition, the Department of Housing and Urban Development (HUD) in early 2011 was backstopping a quarter of all funding for the development of multifamily housing.[4] Along with direct public works spending, federally sponsored entities such as the Federal Housing Administration, Fannie Mae, and Freddie Mac were insuring or guaranteeing about 90% of new home mortgages.[5]

Even with the increased federal activity, much of the construction industry—made up of hundreds of thousands of companies, from mom-and-pop homebuilders to huge, international firms— remains mired in a deep downturn. The jobless rate for construction workers was 20% in March 2011.[6] Housing starts in 2009 and 2010 were the lowest in 50 years.[7] Commercial building plunged 40% between 2006 and 2010. In total, the contraction in construction, both residential and nonresidential, accounted for 16% of the decline in U.S. economic activity in 2009.[8]

While the spike in construction in the early 2000s may not have been sustainable, forecasters generally do not expect construction to begin to recover to more normal, long-run levels until 2012, and it may remain at a lower-than-average pace for some time. Faced with a downbeat outlook, and with stimulus funding winding down, representatives of the various construction segments have asked the 112th Congress to approve additional initiatives to bolster the industry, including an infrastructure bank to finance long-term projects and financial incentives to make commercial buildings more energy-efficient. The requests come as Congress embarks on a far-reaching debate about the appropriate level of federal spending, and is examining the effectiveness of previous initiatives that affect construction and real estate-related sectors. For example, lawmakers are considering how to fund transportation programs, whether to continue foreclosure forbearance programs, and how to restructure Fannie Mae and Freddie Mac.

A bipartisan panel appointed by President Obama, the National Commission on Fiscal Responsibility and Reform, issued a wide-ranging report in December 2010 that proposed limiting the mortgage interest deduction[9] as part of an overhaul of the tax code, which could alter housing demand and prices. It also suggested setting up an infrastructure fund, coupled with changes to transportation spending. These proposals parallel a broader debate about whether U.S. consumers and businesses have been overinvesting in certain areas of real estate, such as housing, thereby distorting investment and hindering the economy,[10] while underfunding other sectors, such as roads, bridges, and other infrastructure. Such proposals, if adopted, would reorder federal support for construction.

This report will outline the structure of the construction industry, and briefly describe congressional initiatives that affect the sector.

THE SHAPE OF THE INDUSTRY

The construction industry is geographically dispersed and largely composed of small businesses. About 90% of U.S. construction companies have 20 or fewer employees, and 80% have 10 or fewer, according to the Census Bureau.[11] However, most construction employees work for the 10% of builders with 20 or more employees. Overall, about a quarter of construction jobs are in residential and commercial construction, with the bulk in the heavy and public works segment.[12] In general, barriers to entry in the construction field are low, though materials and land costs can be volatile; zoning, land use regulations and unique plans needed for individual structures can make projects complex; and financing and bonding are currently tougher to secure. Licensing requirements for specialty and general contractors vary from state to state.[13]

There were about 5.5 million construction wage and salary workers in March 2011, along with about 1.9 million self-employed and family workers. The number of wage and salary employees is nearly 30% below the recent high of 7.7 million in mid-2006 (see **Figure 2**). Roughly 13% of construction workers belong to labor unions, compared to 6.9% of private-sector workers and 11.9% of all U.S. workers.[14] The percentage of construction workers in unions has declined from 17.5% in 2000.

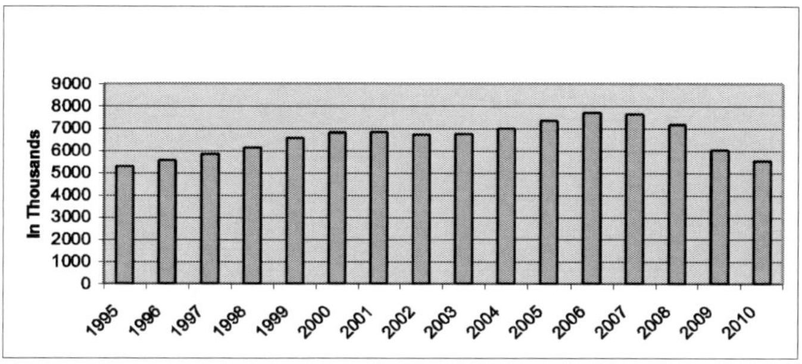

Source: Department of Labor, Bureau of Labor Statistics.

Note: Data are annual averages for private-sector construction workers, age 1 6 and older.

Figure 2. Construction Industry Employment.

Most construction workers are specialty contractors, meaning that they work in a specific area such as carpentry or plumbing and heating.[15] Construction companies rely on managers or general contractors to oversee projects, subletting work to contractors in areas such as drywall, electrical, painting, steel, plumbing, masonry, and roofing.

Construction contracts are generally awarded through a competitive bidding process—which is often required for government projects. Even homeowners doing comparatively small renovations often seek a price from more than one bidder. There is evidence that bidding has become more competitive since the 2007 downturn. A 2010 survey of nearly 1,300 U.S. contractors found that 81% had adjusted bids to leave themselves a smaller profit margin, and 7% had cut bids to the point that they were working at a loss.[16] Labor costs in construction have been rising more slowly than in other industries during the past year,[17] while prices for some materials declined during the recession. But prices for key construction materials in heavy demand globally—including diesel fuel, copper, and lumber—have risen. [18]

Construction firms are trying to bolster their bottom lines by increasing productivity, a measure of output per person. Some large homebuilders, for example, have reduced the number of house plans they offer and introduced new software to improve efficiency. [19] Advances in construction productivity, in general, appear to have lagged many other industries for a number of reasons, however, including the dispersed nature of the sector and the complexity of individual projects— which require financing, design, site preparation, and compliance with zoning, environmental, and other regulations. A 2009 study by the National Research Council (established by the National Academy of Sciences) listed a range of proposals for improving efficiency in the industry.

> Studies focusing on construction efficiency, in contrast to productivity, have documented 25 to 50 percent waste in coordinating labor and in managing, moving, and installing materials ... The sheer number of construction firms ... make[s] it difficult to deploy new technologies, best practices, or other innovations effectively across a critical mass of owners, contractors, and subcontractors.[20]

HOMEBUILDING

Homebuilding is a cyclical sector of the economy, vulnerable to changes in consumer spending, demographics, job growth, and interest rates. Nearly all U.S. recessions since World War II have been preceded by a housing market decline.[21] While housing has tended to lead the economy into downturns, it has also been a key sector aiding in recovery, with housing generally resuming growth six to nine months into recessions.[22] According to the National Association of Home Builders (NAHB), home construction has increased by an average of 28% in the first year of all post-World War II economic recoveries, except for the current cycle, in which it rose by less than 5%.[23] The housing market is hampered by high unemployment in the overall economy, difficulty in securing financing, and a glut of foreclosed and recently built houses currently on the market.

Residential building, which includes detached houses, townhouses, condominiums, and apartments, accounted for about $255 billion of the $792 billion annual value of construction put in place in March 2011.[24] The largest share of homebuilding activity is in the South, followed by the West, Midwest, and Northeast. Geographic differences arise from factors including population growth and availability of land. Homebuilding is subject to seasonal as well as geographic variations. New home construction generally decreases in the winter in the Northeast due to cold and storms. Government agencies and private forecasters adjust their data for such seasonal fluctuations—defined as changes that occur in the same month with similar magnitude and direction each year.

U.S. housing starts averaged about 1.5 million units annually from 1959-2010. Housing starts rose to more than 2 million in 2006, before declining to a historically low 587,000 in 2010.[25] Similarly, U.S. new single-family home sales rose to 1.28 million units in 2005, then fell to 323,000 in 2010—the lowest level since 1963 (see **Figure 3**). Analysts estimate that under more normal economic conditions, builders would erect and renovate 1.5 million housing units annually to meet the needs of a growing population and to replace aging housing stock. Even if the economy enters a period of sustained expansion, it could take two to three years to absorb the excess supply of foreclosed and vacant homes now on the market.[26]

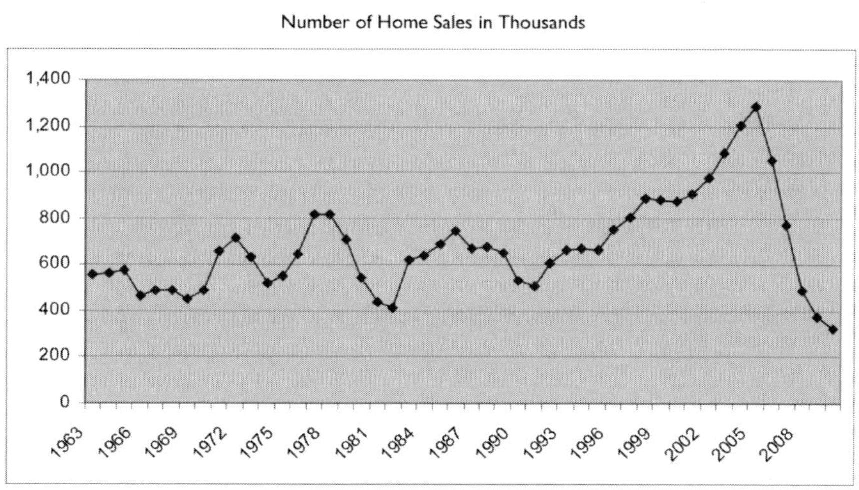

Source: U.S. Census Bureau. Note: Annual data.

Figure 3. Single-Family New Home Sales.

Most homebuilders are small businesses. The NAHB[27] has estimated that more than 65% of homebuilders have annual receipts of less than $1 million, 31% have $1 million to $10 million, and 4.1% bring in more than $10 million. Homebuilding has more startups, and shutdowns, than all other industries.[28] A number of homebuilders have gone out of business or filed for bankruptcy since the peak of the market in 2006. Others have consolidated. Many remaining builders have taken steps to reposition themselves, including laying off workers and halting projects. Some builders and developers have sold land, or have chosen not to exercise options to purchase land at a set price. At the same time, builders in better financial shape have been buying land or partially completed projects from banks and struggling developers, often paying a fraction of the prices that would have been commanded several years ago.[29] Among the largest homebuilders are D.R. Horton, Pulte Homes, Lennar Corp., NVR, KB Home, Hovnanian Enterprises, and the Ryland Group. Publicly traded homebuilders were gaining market share prior to the 2007 recession, but took a financial beating in the past several years (see **Figure 4**).

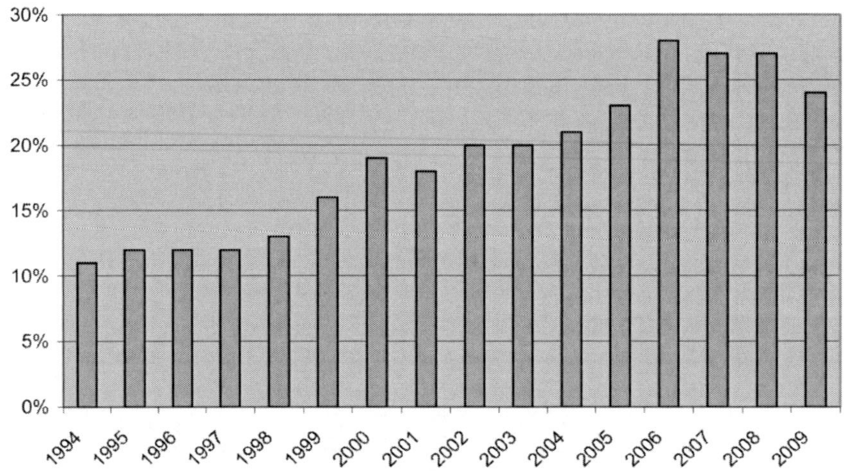

Source: *Builder*, National Association of Home Builders, *Structure of the Home-building Industry.*

Figure 4. Top 10 Homebuilders' Share of Single-Family New Home Sales.

While results vary from firm to firm, a number of homebuilders in recent years found themselves carrying land and unsold inventory, and having a tough time finding homebuyers able to qualify for mortgages. Some firms focused on products geared toward first-time buyers, who were eligible for federal tax credits.[30] In a new twist, large builder Beazer Homes has started a preowned homes division, debuting in Arizona, that will rent houses built since 2004 that have come back on the market via distress sales. The company expects to capitalize on the low prices of homes and the fact that rental properties are at a premium in Phoenix, as would-be buyers cannot secure financing.[31]

Analysts have predicted that large builders could regain market share as the economy improves.[32] Some publicly traded homebuilders are in a better position to weather the downturn than their smaller competitors because of their ability to sell stock and to tap into long-term bank lines of credit. According to Standard & Poor's, large builders have "cash equivalents and unused bank lines of credit facilities that approach $2 billion, with no major debt outstanding maturing before 2011 (or as late as 2013, in some cases)."[33] However, some large firms concentrated their activity in areas such as Phoenix, Las Vegas, and Miami, which are now extremely distressed in terms of foreclosures and excess inventory. That could make it harder for them to expand aggressively as the market recovers.[34]

So far there are few signs that the housing market as a whole is recovering. U.S. housing starts were at a seasonally adjusted annual rate of 549,000 in March 2011. That is 13% below the March 2010 rate of 634,000.[35] Single-family new home sales were running at a seasonally adjusted annual rate of 300,000 during the month, 21.9% below March 2010.[36]

Commercial Construction

Commercial construction generally refers to buildings used to facilitate financial activities or produce income, such as shopping malls, hotels, or office buildings, although the definition can include residential facilities, including apartment buildings and senior living developments. Firms in this segment tend to be larger, with an average of 16 employees, versus four in the homebuilding sector. Some large commercial builders include Fluor Corporation and Foster Wheeler.

Commercial building, like housing, has been subject to periods of boom and bust. Increased demand after World War I, and innovations in financing, gave rise to a commercial real estate boom that produced more skyscrapers from 1922 to 1931 than any 10-year period since—and led to a collapse that contributed to the Great Depression.[37] The United States experienced major commercial real estate contractions in the 1 980s and 1990s after developers financed so-called "see-through" office buildings—speculative structures without pre-leased tenants—prompted in part by changes in federal tax law and policies that allowed savings and loans to concentrate more in commercial real estate lending. [38] More recently, commercial building expanded from the late 1990s through much of the 2000s, with demand arising in concert with ready credit and the housing boom. Firms built shopping malls and other retail and office buildings near new subdivisions. Different areas of the country may have a higher concentration of some types of commercial construction (see **Table 1** and **Figure 1**.)

Table 1 . Ten States with the Largest Commercial Construction Value in 2009

Ranking	Office	Industrial	Warehouse	Retail	All Categories
1	New York	Illinois	Texas	Texas	New York
2	Virginia	Ohio	California	Florida	Texas
3	California	Texas	Florida	California	California
4	Texas	New York	New York	Illinois	Virginia
5	Florida	Arizona	Pennsylvania	New York	Florida
6	N. Carolina	Pennsylvania	Arizona	Georgia	Illinois
7	Washington	California	Georgia	N. Carolina	Ohio
8	Maryland	New Mexico	Ohio	Pennsylvania	Pennsylvania
9	Oklahoma	Louisiana	Washington	Ohio	N. Carolina
10	Washington, DC	Colorado	N. Carolina	Washington	Arizona

Source: NAIOP (the Commercial Real Estate Development Association), McGraw-Hill Construction Analytics, George Mason University Center for Regional Analysis.

Note: The 10 states with the largest construction values accounted for 56% of the construction outlays in the United States, and the top 20 states for 80%.

Like housing, the commercial market is now under stress. The value of privately financed retail, hotel, and office construction declined by more than half from 2008 to 2010. Building of hotels and other lodging plunged by two-thirds during that period.[39] A recent analysis by Morgan Stanley found commercial real estate vacancy rates in 2010 exceeded previous records set during the previous, severe downturn in 1991-1993.[40]

Along with lack of demand due to the slow employment market, problems with financing have been an issue for the commercial sector, particularly for commercial mortgage-backed securities.[41] Losses in commercial mortgage-backed securities are forecast by some analysts to be as high as 9%-12%. By comparison, during the early 1990s, the worst performing groups of mortgages had losses of around 10%.[42] The problems have affected banks, savings institutions, life insurance companies, government-sponsored enterprises, and issuers of commercial mortgage-backed securities, dampening the amount of available capital. The Small Business Administration in February 2011 announced a program, authorized by Congress, to help small companies meet commercial real estate loan payments.[43]

Commercial buildings can be managed and financed through Real Estate Investment Trusts (REITs). In the United States, REITs own approximately $500 billion of commercial real estate assets, or 10%-15% of total U.S. commercial real estate owned by institutions such as pension funds, banks, or insurers.[44] REITs, which were created as a way to allow small investors to venture into commercial real estate, saw share prices decline during the recession, though they have been rebounding as apartment and retail leasing have begun to improve.[45] Demand for rental apartments has increased due to the poor economy and the decline in homebuilding and sales.

There are some signs the market is beginning to revive, with recent sales of high-profile properties in cities including Washington, DC, Boston, New York, and Chicago. But "construction financing is effectively non-existent," according to Morgan Stanley.[46] Though some banks have announced new efforts in the commercial real estate field, Federal Reserve data show the value of commercial banks' real estate loan portfolios continuing to deteriorate into 2011.[47]

Forecasters generally do not see commercial construction recovering for another several years. In California, for example, one analyst predicts a commercial real estate turnaround in 2013.[48]

INDUSTRIAL/HEAVY CONSTRUCTION

The industrial and heavy construction sector builds very large, even multi-billion-dollar projects, including municipal facilities, roads, and energy plants. The segment includes significant national and international general contracting, design, engineering, and management firms.

This is the slice of the construction industry where federal spending plays the most direct role. In addition to privately financed projects, such as power plants, states, cities, and the federal government issue or backstop bonds for public works improvements. Government dollars have recently accounted for a larger share of overall construction spending. Public roads, schools, wastewater treatment plants, and other structures accounted for 40% of the value of ongoing construction activity in 2010, compared to about 20% in the early 2000s.[49] State and local government projects made up most of the public spending, though federal spending grew by about 50% from 2007 to 2010, hitting a historic high in dollar terms in October 2010.

Many private companies contract with the federal and state governments for construction work. A number of large construction companies are among the top 200 federal contractors, as compiled by *Government Executive* magazine.[50]

Overall, public works spending has held up better than other construction sectors during the past several years, due in part to federal stimulus funding. The 2009 ARRA included special federal bond programs, including Qualified School Construction Bonds, Build America Bonds, and Recovery Zone Economic Development Bonds.[51] While many state and local governments have faced severe budget problems since 2008, their spending on major construction is typically financed by long-term bonds and is often not directly affected by stresses on current operating budgets. The largest public works spending categories are highway and street work and other transportation, educational facilities, and sewage and water projects.

One big question is whether public spending will decline as states and the federal government grapple with budget deficits. A National League of Cities survey of 338 city officials in October 2010 found that 69% of those responding were delaying or canceling capital spending to save money.[52] A survey of 13 state transportation departments found a 2% reduction on average in transportation spending for 2011-2012 from 2010-2011 levels, according to the Thompson Research Group. At the same time, the National Governors Association found that at least 10 governors have made transportation a priority for the coming year, suggesting there is some prospect of increased construction activity in that sector.[53]

CONSTRUCTION SECTOR AND THE ECONOMY

Construction historically has experienced wide swings from the top to the bottom of an economic cycle.[54] Still, the current construction downturn is one of the worst on record. U.S. construction spending ended 2010 at the lowest level in a decade.[55] Construction value-added, which measures the industry's contribution to gross domestic product, has been declining since 2006 (**Figure 5**.)

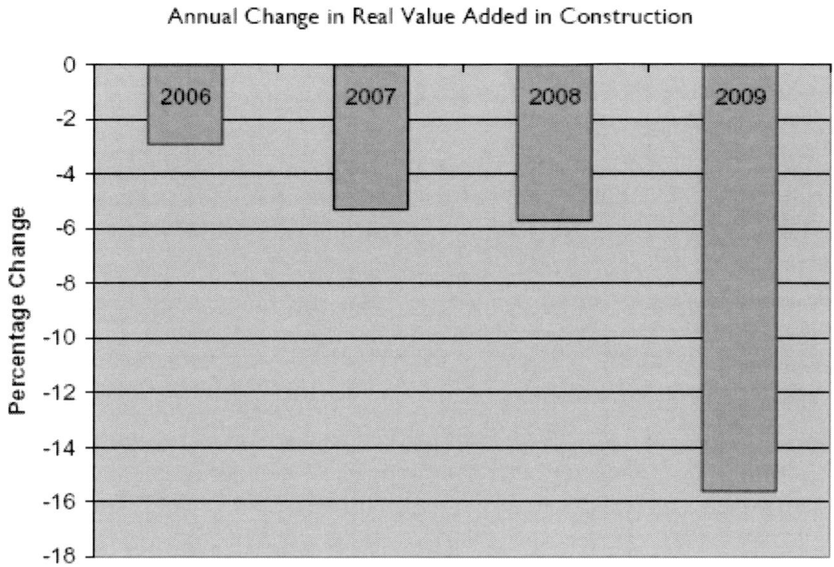

Source: Survey of Current Business, January 2011.
Note: Value-added is a measure of the economic value of construction activity on top of inputs manufactured or produced for the construction sector.

Figure 5. Construction's Contribution to U.S. Economic Growth.

Though the recession that began in December 2007 ended in June 2009, according to the National Bureau of Economic Research (NBER),[56] construction, including housing, has continued to experience job loss and declining investment. That is in contrast to many past recessions, when the housing sector helped lead the U.S. recovery.

The construction slowdown is national in scope, but some areas have been more affected than others. California, Florida, Nevada, Michigan, and Illinois, along with the mountain states, have experienced some of the sharpest declines in building employment and activity. In 2009, the construction drop-off subtracted more than a percentage point of growth from the economies of Nevada, Arizona, and Idaho, and nearly as much in Florida.[57] Global Insight, an economic forecasting firm, says the west coast construction sector is "still a liability, as the housing market refuses to improve."[58]

Construction employment plummeted by 21.4% between December 2007 and August 2009, compared to only 1.1% during the 2001 recession and 7.5% during the 1990-1991 recession.[59] The situation varies by state, but is generally most severe in states that experienced a sharp housing market run-up and steep decline. In Nevada, construction employment plunged from 147,000 in mid-2006 to 57,000 in December 2010. The picture is similar in Florida, where the number of construction workers fell from 686,000 in mid-2006 to 343,000 in December 2010.[60]

Along with construction-specific employment, the Labor Department estimates that the number of workers at architectural firms declined from 220,500 in July 2008 to 150,900 in February 2011.[61] The downturn has had a large impact on Hispanic workers and managers, who constitute a quarter of construction workers—a proportion expected to keep increasing.[62] About 15% of the more than 2 million U.S. firms owned by Hispanics were in the construction field.[63]

There are some bright spots. One area of construction that has increased during the downturn is “green building,” integrated building practices that significantly reduce the environmental footprint of a building in comparison to standard practices.[64] The value of green building starts, while still a small share of the overall market, rose 50% from 2008 to 2010 and made up 25% of new construction.[65]

A variety of factors suggest that the construction industry’s recovery will be gradual. For example, the number of new households formed declined to about 350,000 in 2009 and 2010, below the 1.3 million average of the previous decade and the lowest level since World War II.[66] That decline, probably related to the poor economy, is muting demand for new homes. Employment is still more than 7 million below the 2007 peak, implying that there may be little need for new office space for the next few years. Some members of Congress have indicated that, for budgetary reasons, federal highway spending is unlikely to increase, which could lead to a decline in the amount of highway construction, given rising construction costs. The problems with nuclear reactors in Japan following that country’s recent earthquake and tsunami may lead to the deferral of planned nuclear plants in the United States.

LEGISLATIVE INITIATIVES

Congress has taken a number of actions to spur activity in the various segments of the construction industry. The ARRA included funding for transportation,[67] environment, and energy public works projects; tax changes such as renewable energy credits; money to improve and upgrade federal buildings and defense-related structures;[68] and special construction-related bonds. Congress has enacted three different versions of a homebuyer tax credit since the summer of 2008 to try to make houses more affordable and clear out inventories.[69]

The federal government has bolstered some programs that benefit the construction sector. For example, Housing and Urban Development (HUD) Secretary Shaun Donovan, in a January 2011 speech, noted that the Federal Housing Administration backstopped the development of nearly 150,000 housing units, about 25% of the rental construction market in FY2010, three times as many units as in FY2008.[70]

Homebuilders, construction contractors, and property developers have requested additional federal assistance. Among proposals put forward:

- The Associated General Contractors, which represents a number of larger builders, in March 2011 asked Congress to approve pending trade agreements to boost demand for manufacturing and shipping facilities and to offer tax credits to encourage commercial activity and help contractors invest in equipment.
- The NAHB wants to help homebuilders secure financing for land acquisition, development, and residential construction.[71]
- The U.S. Chamber of Commerce and AFL-CIO have jointly urged lawmakers to pass a transportation bill and invest in infrastructure spending. The current authorization of federal surface transportation programs expired at the end of FY2009, and since then the programs have operated under extensions. The highway trust fund and the revenue sources that feed it have been a reliable mechanism for financing highway and transit programs for five decades, but this is no longer the case. Fuel taxes, which provide most of the money for surface transportation, are unlikely to provide a solid long-term foundation for this desired growth, even if Congress were to raise them modestly. [72]
- On the commercial real estate front, the NAIOP (the Commercial Real Estate Development Organization) wants Congress to make permanent current legislation allowing deductibility of certain building improvements over a 15- year period.[73] The International Council of Shopping Centers is backing legislation to provide federal tax deductions for certain commercial real estate debt payments, and an incentive for investors to purchase underwater properties.[74]

Other issues that could arise relative to construction include long-standing federal Davis-Bacon requirements that employers pay workers at least the locally prevailing wage and fringe benefits on federal construction projects of more than $2,000.[75] Some in the construction sector are urging Congress to nullify Executive Order 13502, signed by President Barack Obama in 2009, which encourages federal agencies "to consider requiring" Project Labor Agreements involving unions on large construction jobs. Whether such changes would increase the overall amount of construction activity is uncertain.

Over the long run, the health of the construction sector depends mainly on the pace of economic growth and job creation, the path of interest rates, the health of the finance sector, and demographics, including immigration and new household formation. In the near term, however, federal action may play a role in determining how quickly construction activity recovers from its depressed state.

End Notes

[1] In addition to direct employment figures, the Labor Department estimates that another 1.9 million people work in construction as sole proprietors or work for family members. That brings total construction employment to about 7.5 million in 2010, for example.

[2] Census Bureau, Construction Spending, Total Construction 1993-2007, http://www.census.gov/const/www/ previousseries.html.

[3] CRS Report R40537, *American Recovery and Reinvestment Act of 2009 (P.L. 111-5): Summary and Legislative History*, by Clinton T. Brass et al.; and CRS Report R40412, *Energy Provisions in the American Recovery and Reinvestment Act of 2009 (P.L. 111-5)*, coordinated by Fred Sissine.

[4] Prepared Remarks of Housing and Urban Development Secretary Shaun Donovan, Real Estate Roundtable State of the Industry Meeting, January 26, 2011, http://portal.hud.gov/hudportal/HUD?src=/press/speeches_remarks_statements/20 1 1/Speech_0126201 1.

[5] Testimony of Susan Wachter, Worley Professor of Financial Management, the Wharton School, Senate Banking Committee, March 9, 2011, http://banking.senate.gov/public/index.cfm?FuseAction=Files.View&FileStore_id= 1bee20b8-d47f-40bc-bdc9-fc0c46f043ee; CRS Report RL34661, *Fannie Mae's and Freddie Mac's Financial Problems*, by N. Eric Weiss. Fannie Mae and Freddie Mac were placed under federal conservatorship in September 2008; U.S. Department of the Treasury and Department of Housing and Urban Development, "Reforming America's Housing Finance Market: A Report to Congress, February 2011, p. 12, http://www.treasury.gov/initiatives/Documents/Reforming%20America%27s%20Housing%20Finance%20Market.pdf.

[6] Department of Labor, Bureau of Labor Statistics, "The Employment Situation—March, 2011," http://bls.gov/ news.release/pdf/empsit.pdf.

[7] Census Bureau, "New Residential Construction: Historic Data," http://www.census.gov/const/www/newresconstindex_excel.html.

[8] Tameka R. L. Harris, William A. Jolliff, Amanda S. Lyndaker, and Matthew B. Schroeder, *Annual Industry Accounts Revised Statistics for 2007–2009*, U.S. Department of Commerce, Bureau of Economic Analsysis, January 2011, http://www.bea.gov/scb/pdf/2011/01January/0111_indy_accts.pdf.

[9]The National Commission on Fiscal Responsibility and Reform, *The Moment of Truth*, December 3, 2010, p. 31, http://www.fiscalcommission.gov/sites/fiscalcommission.gov/files/documents/TheMomentofTruth12_1_2010.pdf.

[10] CRS Report R41596, *Select Tax Benefits for Homeowners: Analysis and Options*, by Mark P. Keightley.

[11] Census Bureau, *2007 Economic Census: Construction Summary Series*, http://factfinder.census.gov/servlet/IBQTable?_bm=y&-geo_id=D&-ds_name=EC0723SG02&-_lang=en.

[12] U.S. Department of Labor, *Career Guide to Industries, 2010-11 Edition*, http://www.bls.gov/oco/cg/cgs003.htm.

[13] National Contractor License Service, http://www.clsi.com/contractor_license.htm; Associated General Contractors of America, State-by-State Listing of Continuing Education License Requirements, https://www.agc.org/cs/ continuing_education_license_requirements.

[14] Department of Labor, Bureau of Labor Statistics, *Union Members Summary*, January 21, 2011, http://www.bls.gov/ news.release/pdf/union2.pdf. The total unionization rate for public-sector workers was more than 36%, while the rate for workers in private industry was 6.9%. Most construction workers are in the private sector.

[15] Department of Labor, Bureau of Labor Statistics, *Career Guide to Industries, 2010-1 1 Edition: Construction,* http://www.bls.gov/oco/cg/cgs003.htm.

[16] Associated General Contractors, "The 2011 Construction Hiring and Business Outlook," http://news.agc.org/wpcontent/uploads/201 1/01/Outlook-Report.pdf.

[17] Department of Labor, Bureau of Labor Statistics, *Employment Cost Index*, December 2010, http://www.bls.gov/ news.release/eci.t0 1 .htm.

[18] Department of Labor, Bureau of Labor Statistics, "Producer Price Indexes—January, 2011," February 16, 2011, http://bls.gov/news.release/pdf/ppi.pdf; Alex Carrick, "RSMeans detects a speed-up in construction material prices," *Reed Construction Data*, March 7, 2011, http://www.reedconstructiondata.com/construction-forecast/news/2011/03/ rsmeans-detects-a-speed-up-in-construction-material-prices/.

[19] John Caulfield, "Heroic Effort," *Builder*, May 2010, http://www.builderonline.com/business/heroic-effort.aspx? page=3.

[20] National Research Council, *Advancing the Competitiveness and Efficiency of the U.S. Construction Industry*, The National Academies Press, 2009, International Standard Book Number-13: 978-0-309-14191-8, p. 2. The National Institute of Standards and Technology (NIST) in 2008 asked the National Research Council (NRC) to appoint a committee of experts to identify ways to improve productivity in the U.S. construction industry. The report arose from that project.

[21] Edward Leamer, *Housing Is the Business Cycle*, National Bureau of Economic Research, Working Paper 13428, September 2007, http://www.nber.org/papers/w13428.pdf?new_window=1.

[22] Ibid.

[23] Testimony of David Crowe, Chief Economist of the National Association of Home Builders, Senate Banking Committee, March 9, 2011, http://banking.senate.gov/public/index.cfm?FuseAction=Hearings.Hearing&Hearing_ID= abfc976f-f14f-46a9-807f-f1b0cd1b71 8e.

[24] Monthly figures at a seasonally adjusted annual rate.

[25] Census Bureau, New Residential Construction, Historic Data, http://www.census.gov/const/www/newresconstindex_excel.html. Housing starts figures include dwellings with up to four units. Single family housing starts, which make up the bulk of housing starts, rose to 1.7 million in 2006, before declining to 471,000 units in 2010.

[26] Testimony of Susan Wachter, Worley Professor of Financial Management, the Wharton School, Senate Banking Committee, March 9, 2011, http://banking.senate.gov/public/index.cfm?FuseAction=Files.View&FileStore_id=1bee20b8-d47f-40bc-bdc9-fc0c46f043ee.

[27] National Association of Home Builders, "NAHB Report Finds Small Builders are the Mainstay of the Nation's Housing Industry," December 21, 2010.

[28] Stephen Melman, *Structure of the Home Building Industry*, National Association of Home Builders, December 1, 2010, http://webcache.googleusercontent.com/search?q=cache:dZ4beV5CCI4J:www.nahb.org/generic.aspx%3FgenericContentID%3D148743+homebuilding+industry+consolidation+U.S.+federal+policy&cd=1&hl=en&ct=clnk&gl=us&source=www.google.com.

[29] Prashant Gopal and John Gittelsohn, "Homebuilders Revive Stalled U.S. Projects as Banks Unload Lots," *Bloomberg*, September 8, 2010, http://noir.bloomberg.com/apps/news?pid=newsarchive&sid=awfdI1fLGMJs; Teresa Burney, "WCI Sells Developments, Pays Off Debt; Toll Brothers purchases WCI community in Florida for $27 million and one in Connecticut for $23.5 million," *Builder*, November 22, 2010, http://www.builderonline.com/landacquisition/wci-sells-developments-pays-off-debt.aspx.

[30] John Caufiled, "Heroic Effort," *Builder*, May 2010, http://www.builderonline.com/business/heroic-effort.aspx?page= 1.

[31] Beazer Homes, "Beazer Homes Introduces Its Pre-Owned Homes Division," *Business Wire*, April 4, 2011, http://ir.beazer.com/phoenix.zhtml?c=98372&p=irol-newsArticle&ID=1526115&highlight=.

[32] John Gittelson, "Biggest Builders to Gain Market Share as Demand Rises," *Bloomberg*, January 19, 2011, http://noir.bloomberg.com/apps/news?pid=newsarchive&sid=aNZKo75DJP.k.

[33] Kenneth Leon, *Industry Surveys: Homebuilding*, Standard & Poor's, January 6, 2011, pp. 2-3.

[34] Stephen Melman, *Structure of the Home Building Industry*, National Association of Home Builders, December 1, 2010.

[35] Census Bureau, "New Residential Construction in March 2011," April 19, 2011, http://www.census.gov/const/ newresconst.pdf.

[36] Census Bureau, "New Residential Sales in March 2011," April 25, 2011, http://www.census.gov/const/ newressales.pdf.

[37] William N. Goetzmann and Frank Newman, *Securitization in the 1920's*, National Bureau of Economic Research, Working Paper 15650, p. 3, http://www.nber.org/papers/w15650.

[38] Federal Deposit Insurance Corp., *The S&L Crisis: A Chrono-Bibliography*, http://www.fdic.gov/bank/historical/ s%26l/index.html.

[39] Census Bureau, "Annual Value of Construction Put in Place, 2002-2010." The Census Bureau value of construction is a measure of the value of construction installed or erected on a site during the measurement period, including cost of materials, labor, contractor profit, architectural and engineering work, taxes, and other miscellaneous costs. For definition see "Definitions of Construction," http://www.census.gov/const/C30/definitions.pdf.

[40] Richard Parkus and Andy Bernard, *CMBS Market Insights*, Morgan Stanley, December 6, 2010, p. 14, http://cop.senate.gov/documents/testimony-020411-parkus.pdf.

[41] CRS Report R41046, *Commercial and Residential Mortgages*, by N. Eric Weiss.

[42] Ibid.

[43] Small Business Administration, "SBA Launches Temporary Program for Commercial Real Estate Refinancing," February 17, 2011, http://www.sba.gov/content/sba-launches-temporary-program-commercial-real-estate-refinancing.

[44] Reit.com, *Reitwatch*, January 2011, http://returns.reit.com/reitwatch/rw1101.pdf. REITs are required to, among other things, invest at least 75% of total assets in real estate and distribute at least 90% of taxable income to shareholders as dividends each year.

[45] Robert McMillan and Royal Shepard, *Industry Surveys: Real Estate Investment Trusts*, Standard & Poor's, December 16, 2010.

[46] Richard Parkus and Andy Bernard, "CMBS Market Insights CRE Debt Markets: Challenges and Opportunities," Morgan Stanley, December 6, 2010, http://cop.senate.gov/documents/testimony-020411-parkus.pdf.

[47] Federal Reserve Board, "Assets and Liabilities of Commercial Banks in the United States," April 8, 2011, http://federalreserve.gov/releases/h8/current/h8.pdf.

[48] Allen Matkins/UCLA Anderson Forecast, "California Commercial Real Estate Survey, February 3, 2011, http://www.uclaforecast.com/allenmatkinsCRES/2011/amcres_survey results_jan11.pdf.

[49] Census Bureau, Value of Construction Put in Place, Annual Data, http://www.census.gov/const/C30/ototal.pdf. The Census Bureau data are a measure of the value of construction installed or erected on a site during the measurement period, including cost of materials, labor, contractor profit, architectural and engineering work, taxes, and other miscellaneous costs.

[50] *Government Executive*, "Top 200 Federal Contractors," August 15, 2010, http://www.govexec.com/features/0810-15/ 0810-15s1s1.htm.

[51] CRS Report R40523, *Tax Credit Bonds: Overview and Analysis*, by Steven Maguire.

[52] Christopher Hoene and Michael Pagano1, *City Fiscal Conditions in 2010*, National League of Cities Research Brief on America's Cities, October 2010, http://www.nlc.org/ASSETS/AE 2679331 8A645C795C9CD11DAB3B39B/ RB_CityFiscalConditions2010.pdf. 1. Cuts in infrastructure were second only to reductions in personnel, used by 79% of surveyed cities to close budget deficits.

[53] National Governors Association, *Interim Analysis: 2011 State of the State Addresses*, http:// www.nga.org/Files/pdf/ SOTSINTERIMANALYSIS201 1 .PDF.

[54] Alex Carrick, RCD Chief Economist, *A New Version of Cyclical Instability in Construction*, http://www.reedconstructiondata.com/alex-carrick/post/a-new-version-of-cyclicalinstability -in-construction/.

[55] Ibid.

[56] National Bureau of Economic Research, "U.S. Business Cycle Expansions and Contractions," http://www.reedconstructiondata.com/alex-carrick/post/a-new-version-of-cyclicalinstability -inconstruction/http://www.nber.org/cycles/US_Business_Cycle_Expansions_and_ Contractions_20100920.pdf. The NBER defines a recession as "a period of falling economic activity spread across the economy, lasting more than a few months, normally visible in real GDP, real income, employment, industrial production, and wholesale-retail sales. The trough marks the end of the declining phase and the start of the rising phase of the business cycle. Economic activity is typically below normal in the early stages of an expansion, and it sometimes remains so well into the expansion."

[57] Department of Commerce, Bureau of Labor Statistics, "Economic Downturn Widespread Among States in 2009," New Release, November 18, 2010, http://www.bea.gov/ newsreleases/regional/gdp_state/2010/gsp1110.htm.

[58] Global Insight, *Pacific Region Executive Summary*, March 10, 2011.

[59] CRS Report R41179, *Long-Term Unemployment and Recessions*, by Gerald Mayer and Linda Levine.

[60] Department of Labor, Bureau of Labor Statistics, *State and Local Employment*. Figures are not seasonally adjusted. The Bureau of Labor Statistics tracks construction employment using a classification system based on construction-ofbuilding contractors, heavy-and-civil engineering construction contractors, and specialty trade contractors. Construction-of-building contractors build residential, industrial, and commercial buildings. Heavy-and-civil engineering construction contractors are involved in building sewers, roads, highways, bridges, tunnels, and other types of heavy-construction projects. Specialty trade contractors are activities such as carpentry, painting, plumbing, and electrical work.

[61] Department of Labor, Bureau of Labor Statistics, *Current Population Survey, Employment, Earnings and Hours*, Architectural Services.

[62] Department of Labor, Bureau of Labor Statistics, *Current Population Survey, Household Data*, Annual Averages, http://www.bls.gov/cps/cpsaat18.pdf; Silver Lake Media Group, *Constru-Guía al Día*, 2011 Media Kit, http://www.cgaldia.com/pdf/CPF_0085_CGAD_2010Media KitAlt_Online.pdf.

[63] Census Bureau, *Survey of Business Owners: Hispanic-Owned Firms: 2007*, http://www.census.gov/econ/sbo/ get07sof.html?1 1.

[64] CRS Report R40147, *Issues in Green Building and the Federal Response: An Introduction*, by Eric A. Fischer.

[65] McGraw-Hill, "Green Building Market Grows 50% in Two Years Despite Recession, Says McGraw Hill Construction Report, November 12, 2010, http://www.facebook.com/topic.php?uid=178850338793522&topic=383.

[66] IHS Global Insight, "U.S. Household Formation is at a Record Low," October 7, 2010.

[67] CRS Report R40214, *Transportation and Transportation Security Related Provisions of House and Senate Stimulus Legislation (H.R. 1)*, by John W. Fischer et al.

[68] CRS Report R40216, *Water Infrastructure Funding in the American Recovery and Reinvestment Act of 2009*, by Claudia Copeland, Megan Stubbs, and Charles V. Stern.

[69] CRS Report R40955, *An Economic Analysis of the Homebuyer Tax Credit*, by Mark P. Keightley.

[70] Prepared Remarks of Secretary Shaun Donovan, Real Estate Roundtable State of the Industry Meeting, January 26, 2011, http://portal.hud.gov/hudportal/HUD?src=/press/speeches_remarks_statements/2011/Speech_01262011.

[71] National Association of Home Builders, "Housing Production Credit Crisis," http://www.nahb.org/fileUpload_details.aspx?contentTypeID=3&contentID=136393&subContentID=328744.

[72] CRS Report R415 12, *Surface Transportation Program Reauthorization Issues for the 112th Congress*, coordinated by Robert S. Kirk.

[73] Chris McAdams, "Stimulus spending on highways isn't delivering on job promises," *McClatchy Newspapers*, September 26, 2010, http://www.mcclatchydc.com/2010/09/26/101055/stimulus-spending-on-highways.html.

[74] International Council of Shopping Centers,"ICSC Supports CRE Act, Tax Legislation to Jumpstart Commercial Real Estate," March 17, 2011, http://www.icsc.org/apps/news_item.phpid=2746.

[75] CRS Report R40663, The Davis-Bacon Act and Changes in Prevailing Wage Rates, 2000 to 2008, by Gerald Mayer.

In: The Construction Sector in the U.S. Economy ISBN 978-1-61942-893-5
Editors: N. M. McDonald et al.

Chapter 2

CONSTRUCTION EMPLOYMENT: A VISUAL ESSAY*

Benjamin Cover

Construction occupations accounted for 4.9 million jobs in May 2010, down from 6.5 million in May 2006 when employment in construction-related occupations reached a peak. Since then, employment has declined among establishments whose primary output was construction or construction trade services and among workers performing construction-related activities in any industry. Employment in 40 of the 46 construction occupations decreased over this time, with some occupations declining by half. The employment declines were more extreme in some industries than others. Employment declines were often steeper among the lower-paid construction helper occupations.

U.S. average wages for construction occupations in May 2010 were $21.12 per hour, about the same as the all-occupations average of $21.35. Between May 2006 and May 2010, average hourly wages grew 2.7 percent per year for construction occupations, less than the 3.2-percent growth in hourly wages for all occupations.

This visual essay examines employment and wages of workers in construction occupations in May 2010, when construction employment was at its lowest point in over a decade. Some comparisons are made with employment and earnings in May 2006.

---

* This is an edited, reformatted and augmented version of an piece in the *Monthly Labor Review* dated Novermber 2011.

The Occupational Employment Statistics survey is a survey of 1.2 million business establishments conducted in six semiannual panels over a 3-year period. Respondents are asked to list the occupation and wage range for each of their employees. Data from the six most recent panels are used each year to provide wage and employment estimates for about 800 occupations by area and industry.

This essay was prepared by Benjamin Cover, an economist in the Office of Employment and Unemployment Statistics, Bureau of Labor Statistics.

1. Employment and Mean Hourly Wages for Workers in the 10 Largest Construction Occupations, May 2010

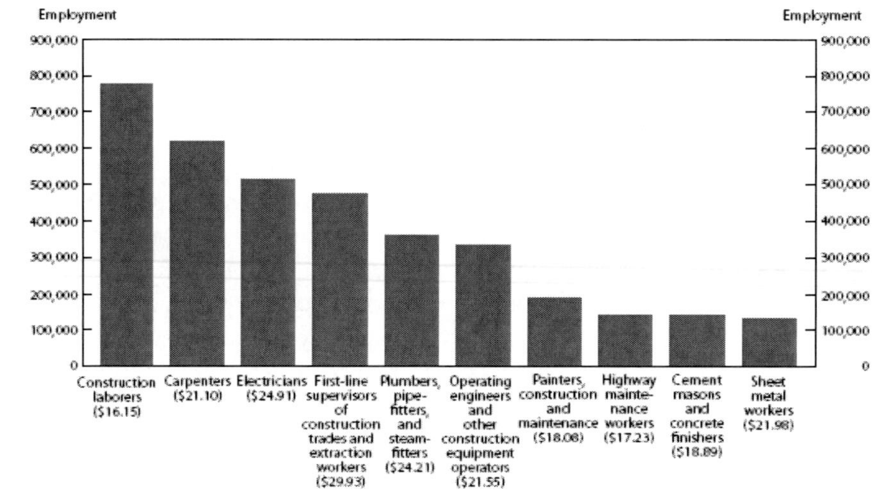

Source: U.S. Bureau of Labor Statistics.

- Most of the largest construction occupations were the construction trades workers.
- The 10 occupations shown accounted for more than 76 percent of employment in construction occupations in May 2010.
- Construction laborers had the lowest wage among the 10 largest construction occupations.

- First-line supervisors of construction trades and extraction workers had the highest wage among the 10 largest construction occupations.

2. Construction Occupations with the Highest Mean Hourly Wages, May 2010

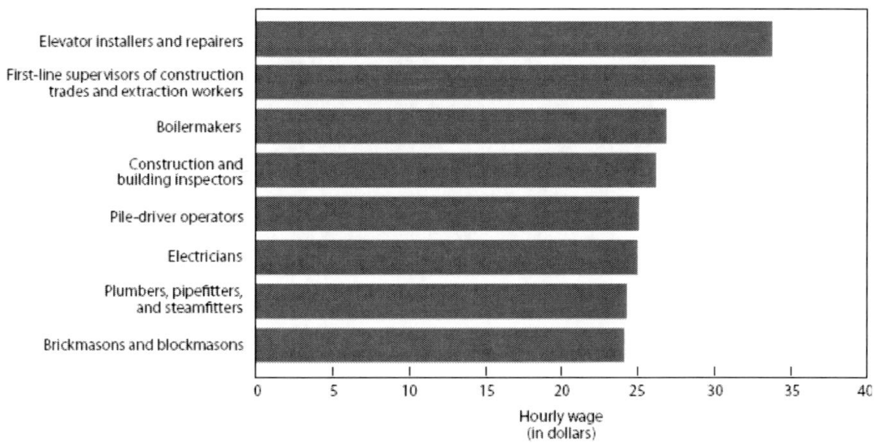

Source: U.S. Bureau of Labor Statistics.

- Construction workers earned an average of $21.12 per hour in May 2010, about the same as the overall mean for all occupatio ns.
- The eight highest paid construction occupations were specialized construction trade workers or their supervisors.
- Earning an average hourly wage of $33.66, elevator installers and repairers had the highest wage among construction workers in May 2010.
- Three of the construction occupations with the highest wages were also among the 10 largest construction occupations—first-line supervisors of construction trades and extraction workers, electricians, and plumbers, pipefitters, and steamfitters.
- With 4,230 workers in May 2010, pile-driver operators was the smallest of the high-paying construction occupations.

3. Change in Mean Hourly Wages in Construction Occupations with the Largest Percent Decrease in Employment, May 2006–May 2010

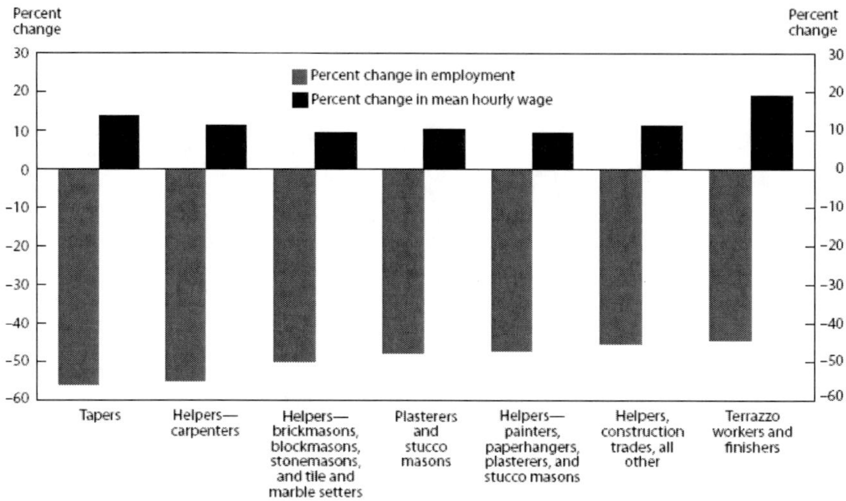

Source: U.S. Bureau of Labor Statistics.

- Employment decreased in 40 of the 46 construction occupations between May 2006 and May 2010.
- Overall, employment in construction occupations decreased 25 percent between May 2006 and May 2010.
- Four of the construction occupations with the largest percent decrease in employment between May 2006 and May 2010 were various helpers of construction trade workers.
- Employment for tapers and carpenter helpers fell by more than 50 percent. The employment decline was 22,400 for tapers and 57,290 for carpenter helpers.
- The average hourly wage in construction occupations grew 11 percent between May 2006 and May 2010, an average annual increase of 2.7 percent, slightly lower than the increase of 13 percent, or 3.2 percent per year, for all occupations.

- Hourly wage changes for the construction occupations with the largest percent decline in employment were similar to the average for total construction occupations.
- With a 37-percent decrease in employment over the 4-year period, carpenters experienced a smaller percent decrease than the occupations shown but had the largest overall decline in jobs, which fell by 365,580.

4. Construction Occupations with the Largest Increase in Employment, May 2006–May 2010

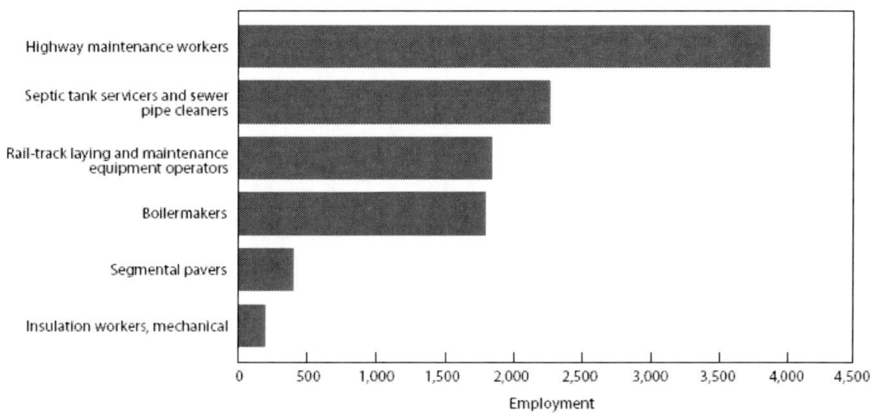

Source: U.S. Bureau of Labor Statistics.

- Construction occupations that grew tended to be smaller occupations and were not related to new building construction.
- Employment for highway maintenance workers increased from 138,670 in May 2006 to 142,530 in May 2010.
- The increase in average hourly wages over the 4-year period for the occupations shown ranged from 2.1 percent for mechanical insulation workers to 16.6 percent for rail-track laying and maintenance equipment operators.

5. Change in Employment and Wages in States with the Largest Percent Employment Decrease in Construction Occupations, May 2006–May 2010

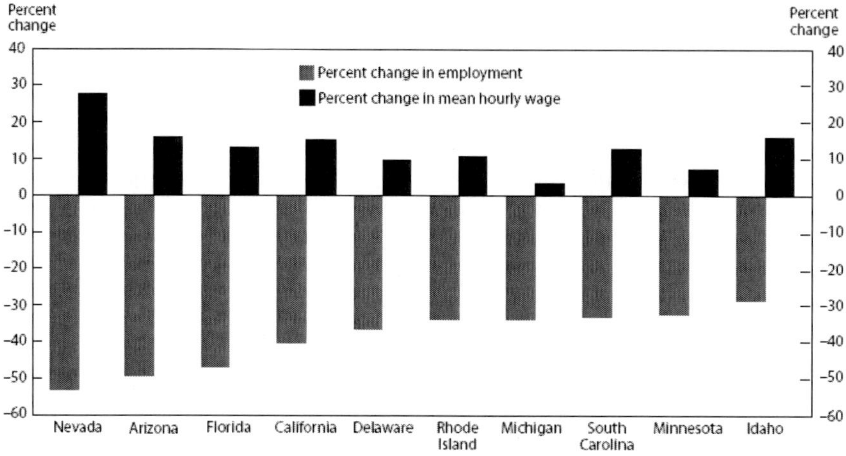

Source: U.S. Bureau of Labor Statistics.

- Nevada had the largest percent decrease in construction occupations employment and the largest increase in mean wages for construction occupations from May 2006 to May 2010.
- Average hourly wages for detailed occupations may increase because of wage increases for individual workers or because lower paid workers are let go, while higher wage workers are retained.
- In Nevada, mean hourly wages for construction occupations had an annual average increase of 6.3 percent from May 2006 to May 2010.
- Part of the wage increase in Nevada was due to employment declining in helper occupations and rising in higher paying occupations, such as elevator installers and repairers.
- With a decline of 41 percent, California had the largest absolute decrease of employment in construction occupations from 815,510 in May 2006 to 485,120 in May 2010.

- Carpenter helpers had one of the largest declines in employment in all the States shown.

6. Change in Employment and Wages in the States with an Increase in Construction Occupations Employment, May 2006–May 2010

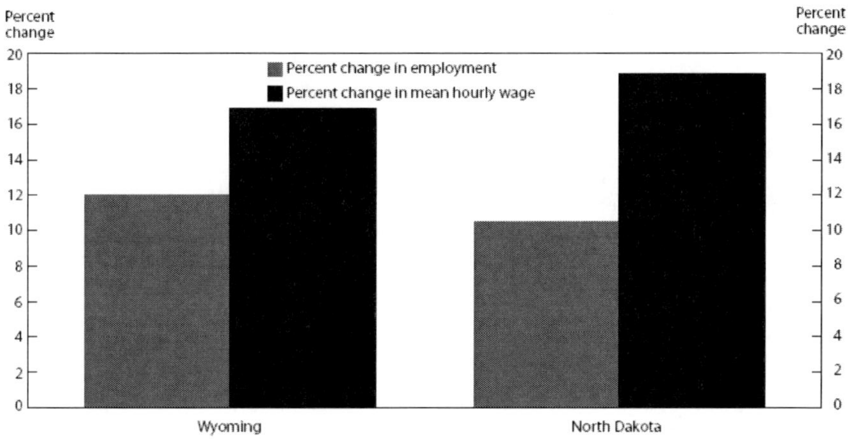

Source: U.S. Bureau of Labor Statistics.

- Employment in construction occupations grew in only two states from May 2006 to May 2010.
- The increase of employment in construction occupations came from increases in different occupations in each of the two states.
- In North Dakota, employment for highway maintenance workers increased more than 65 percent. The occupation with the largest absolute increase in employment in North Dakota was first-line supervisors of construction trades and extraction workers.
- Operating engineers and other construction equipment operators and electricians contributed to the increase in employment for Wyoming.
- The growth in hourly wages for construction occupations in Wyoming and North Dakota was above the nationwide average.

7. Change in Employment and Wages in Metropolitan Areas with the Largest Percent Employment Decrease in Construction Occupations, May 2006–May 2010

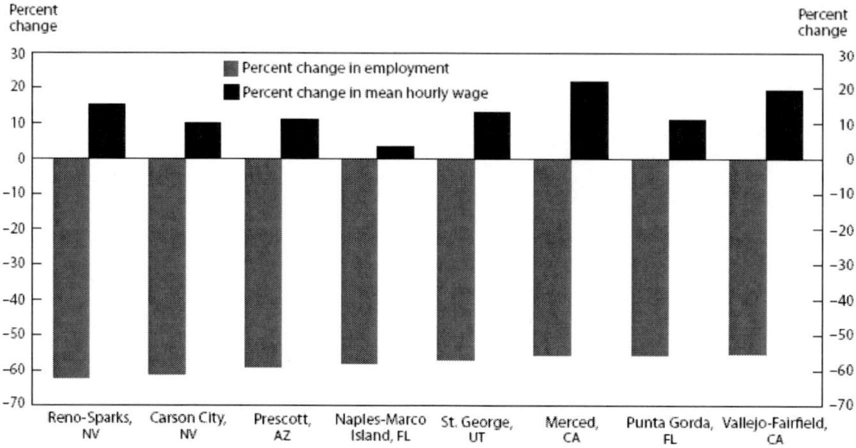

Source: U.S. Bureau of Labor Statistics.

- Nine metropolitan areas in California, six metropolitan areas in Florida, and three metropolitan areas in Nevada showed at least a 50-percent decrease in employment in construction occupations from May 2006 to May 2010; the areas with the steepest employment declines in those states were Merced and Vallejo- Fairfield in California and Naples-Marco Island and Punta Gorda in Florida.
- Employment in construction occupations fell more than 60 percent from May 2006 to May 2010 in Reno- Sparks, NV, and Carson City, NV.
- Employment in construction occupations decreased more than 50 percent in Las Vegas, NV. Wages for construction occupations in Las Vegas, however, increased more than 30 percent.
- Construction hourly wages increased in each of the areas shown during the May 2006–May 2010 period, ranging from 3.4 percent in Naples-Marco Island, FL, to 22.1 percent in Merced, CA.

8. Change in Employment and Wages in the Metropolitan Areas with at Least a 15–percent Employment increase in Construction Occupations, May 2006–May 2010

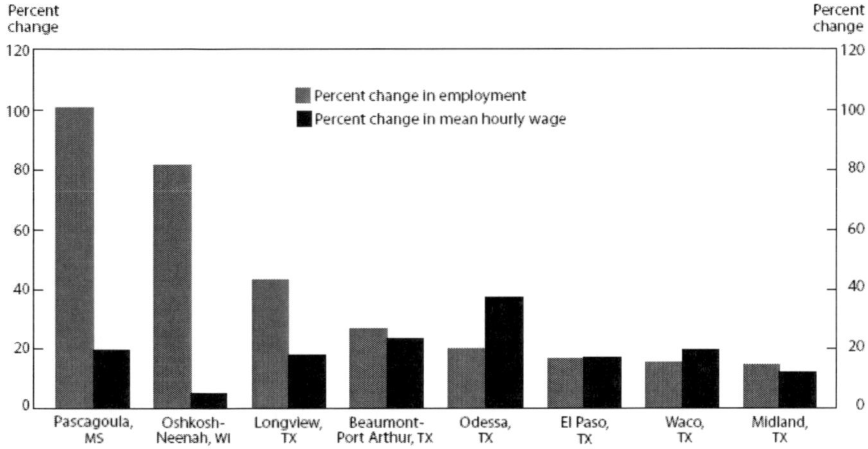

Source: U.S. Bureau of Labor Statistics.

- Employment in construction occupations more than doubled in Pascagoula, MS, and increased by more than 80 percent in Oshkosh-Neenah, WI, from May 2006 to May 2010.
- Employment increased in 20 out of 25 construction occupations in Pascagoula, MS.
- Although the overall employment in construction occupations decreased by 1 percent in Texas from May 2006 to May 2010, employment increased in 13 of the State's 26 metropolitan areas.
- Nearly all the areas with substantial employment growth in construction occupations also had above the U.S. average wage growth from May 2006 to May 2010. The sole exception was Oshkosh-Neenah, WI, where wages grew by only 5 percent.

9. Construction Occupations in the San Francisco-San Mateo-Redwood City, CA, Metropolitan Division with Mean Wages at least 55 Percent Higher than the National Average for that Occupation, May 2010

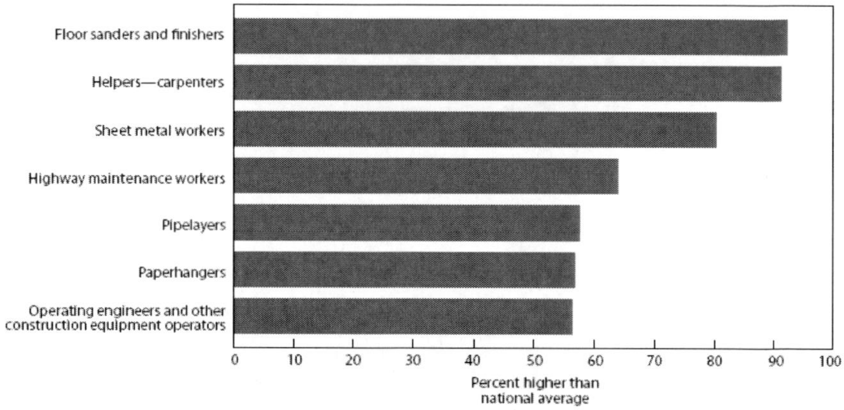

Source: U.S. Bureau of Labor Statistics.

- The San Francisco-San Mateo-Redwood City, CA, metropolitan division had the highest mean wage in May 2010 for construction workers at $30.14.
- The San Francisco-San Mateo-Redwood City, CA, metropolitan division had above average hourly wages for all occupation groups, but construction occupations had the highest wage premium of all the major occupational groups.
- Floor sanders and finishers and carpenter helpers in San Francisco-San Mateo-Redwood City earned almost twice the national average hourly wage for their occupation.
- Most occupations in this metropolitan division with the highest wage premiums were construction trade occupations. With the exception of carpenter helpers, most helper occupations had a below average premium.
- Although the wages for construction occupations were higher, on average, in the San Francisco-San Mateo-Redwood City, CA,

metropolitan division, employment in construction occupations accounted for a relatively small share of the area's overall employment. Construction occupations accounted for 4 percent of employment nationwide and 3 percent in San Francisco-San Mateo-Redwood City.

10. Location Quotients for Construction Occupations in Pascagoula, MS, May 2010

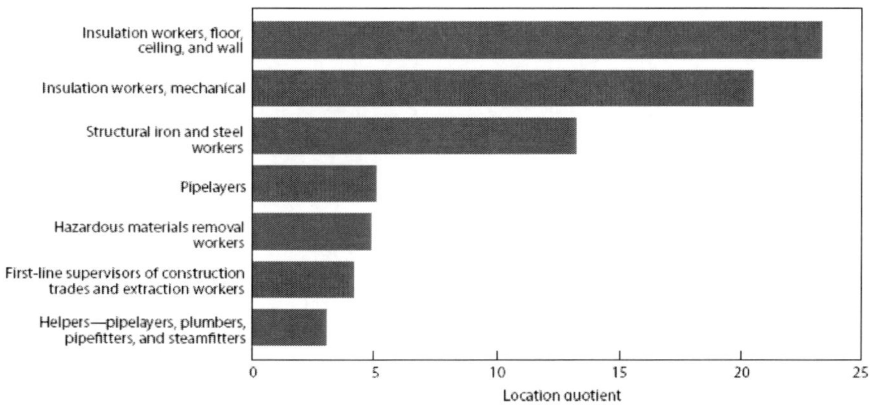

Source: U.S. Bureau of Labor Statistics.

- Pascagoula, MS, had a larger share of its employment in construction occupations than did any other metropolitan area in the United States, with over three times the national average.
- The concentration of employment in every construction occupation in Pascagoula, MS, was higher than the national average, with the exception of highway maintenance workers.
- At $19.07, the mean wage for construction occupations in Pascagoula, MS, was below the U.S. average for construction occupations at $21.12.
- Of the occupations shown, only helpers—pipelayers, plumbers, pipefitters, and steamfitters had a mean hourly wage higher than the U.S. average for that occupation.

11. Change in Employment and Mean Hourly Wages for Construction Occupations in the Residential and Nonresidential Building Construction Industries, May 2006–May 2010

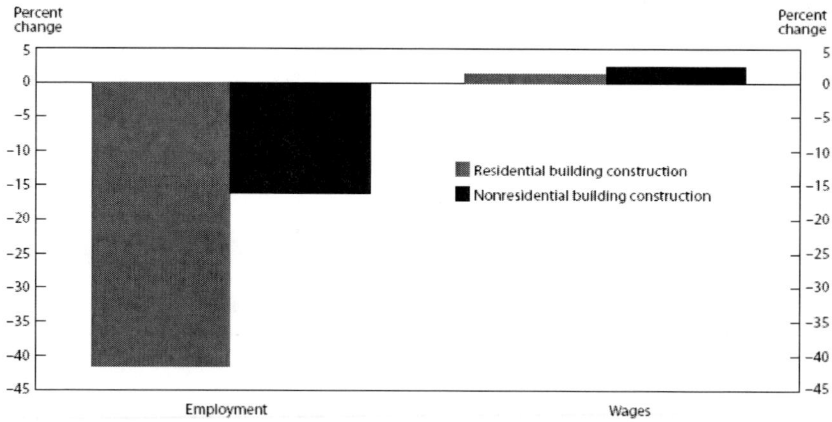

Source: U.S. Bureau of Labor Statistics.

- Residential construction occupations had a larger employment decline and lower hourly wage growth than did nonresidential construction occupations.
- From May 2006 to May 2010, employment declined 42 percent in residential construction, compared with 16 percent in nonresidential construction.
- Employment in the largest construction occupation, carpenters, decreased 45 percent in residential construction compared with 23 percent in nonresidential construction.
- The average annual hourly wage growth from May 2006 to May 2010 was 1.8 percent in residential construction and 2.7 percent in nonresidential construction compared with 3.2 percent for all industries combined.

12. Employment in the Largest occupations in the Building Construction Subsector, by Residential and Nonresidential Industry Group, May 2010

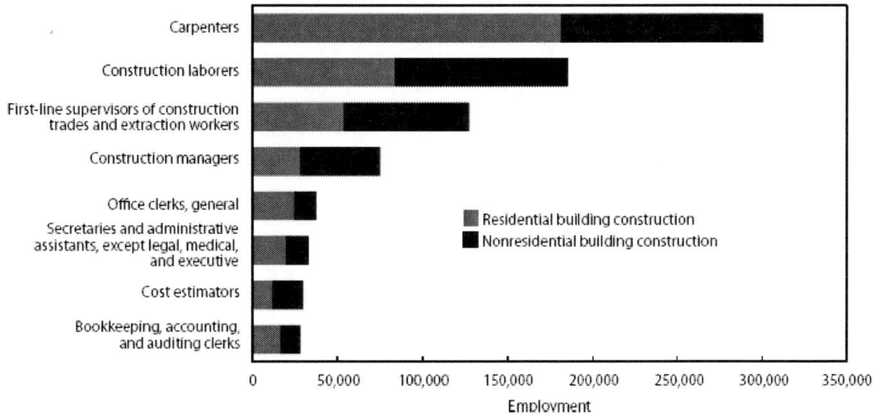

Source: U.S. Bureau of Labor Statistics.

- Construction occupations accounted for 64 percent of employment in residential building construction and 62 percent of employment in nonresidential building construction.
- Carpenters made up almost half of the construction occupation employment in residential building construction but accounted for less than a third of the nonresidential building construction employment.
- First-line supervisors of construction trades and extraction workers and construction managers were more prevalent in nonresidential building construction than in residential building construction, accounting for about 4 percentage points more of the overall construction occupations employment.

13. Mean Hourly Wages for the Largest Occupations in the Building Construction Subsector, by Residential and Nonresidential Industry Group, May 2010

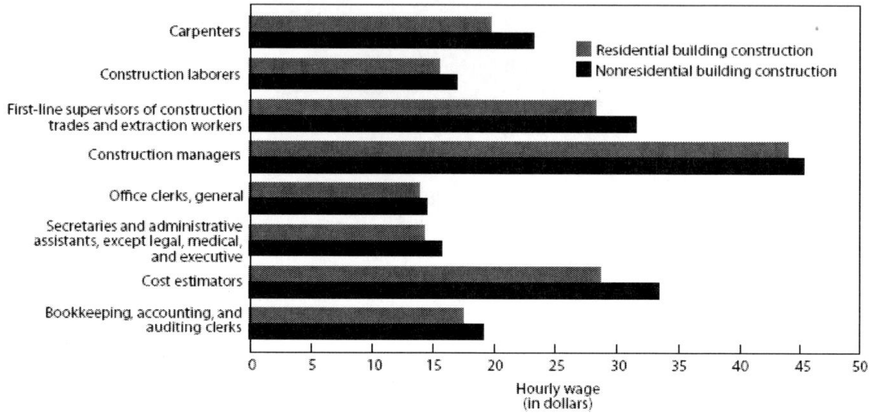

Source: U.S. Bureau of Labor Statistics.

- Wages were consistently higher among workers in nonresidential building construction than those in residential building construction.
- The mean hourly wage for construction occupations was $19.55 in residential building construction, compared with $22.64 in nonresidential building construction.
- Cost estimators had the largest nominal difference in mean hourly wages with a $4.74 spread between nonresidential and residential building construction.
- Carpenters had the largest percent difference in mean hourly wages—17.6 percent—between nonresidential and residential building construction.

In: The Construction Sector in the U.S. Economy ISBN 978-1-61942-893-5
Editors: N. M. McDonald et al.

Chapter 3

CONSTRUCTION EMPLOYMENT PEAKS BEFORE THE RECESSION AND FALLS SHARPLY THROUGHOUT IT*

Adam Hadi

Construction employment fell by 1.5 million[1] during the December 2007–June 2009 recession,[2] bringing employment in the industry to the lowest level since March 1998. The losses during the recession represented a 19.8-percent decline in construction employment, the largest percent decline of any nonfarm industry supersector. The majority of the losses came during the last 9 months of the recession, when employment declined by 1 million. (See chart 1.) Job losses averaged 49,000 per month between December 2007 and September 2008 and then accelerated to an average of 115,000 per month through June 2009. Those construction firms which engaged primarily in residential construction activities started losing jobs more than a year before the recession started, and those firms which conducted primarily nonresidential and heavy construction projects did not start losing jobs until the onset of recession.

---

* This is an edited, reformatted and augmented version of a piece in the *Monthly Labor Reivew* dated April 2011.

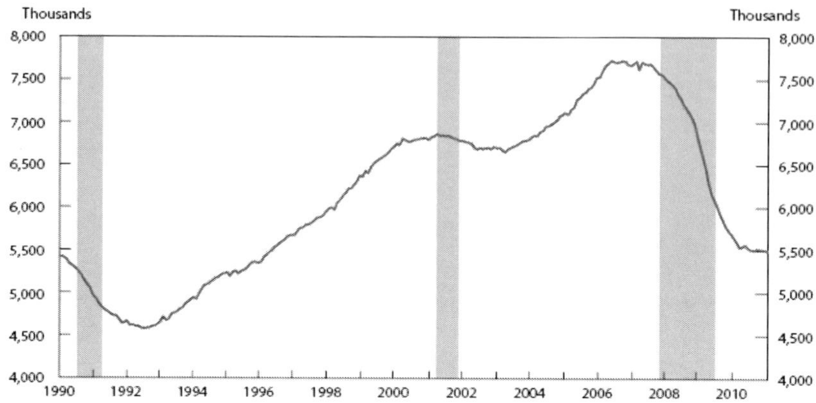

Note: Shaded areas represent recessions as determined by the National Bureau of Economic Research.

Source: U.S. Bureau of Labor Statistics.

Chart 1. Construction employment, 1990–2010, monthly data, seasonally adjusted.

LOSSES IN RESIDENTIAL CONSTRUCTION

In 2005, demand for residential construction peaked and the U.S. housing market started experiencing the beginnings of an unprecedented downturn. Deep employment losses in residential building construction and among residential specialty trade contractors started in 2006, worsened during the recession, and continued at a slower pace after the recession ended in June 2009. (Residential building construction and residential specialty trade contractors are analyzed together as “residential construction” in this article.)

Residential construction employment peaked in April 2006 at 3.5 million jobs, following approximately 5 years of rapid growth. This expansionary period roughly coincided with a housing bubble in the United States during which home prices rose greatly, peaking in April 2006 as employment in residential construction did.[3] New home sales,[4] housing starts,[5] and the Housing Market Index[6] all peaked between mid- 2005 and early 2006. (See chart 2.) Employment in residential construction dropped rapidly during the second half of 2006 as the housing market worsened. Delinquencies in mortgage payments began to rise, particularly for nontraditional loans, and by the beginning of the recession in December 2007, residential construction employment had fallen by 390,000, or 11 percent. Other housing indicators also plummeted from their prerecession peaks.

Note: Shaded areas represent recessions as determined by the National Bureau of Economic Research.

Sources: New home sales and housing starts data are from the U.S. Census Bureau, and Housing Market Index data are from the National Association of Home Builders.

Chart 2. New home sales, housing starts, and the Housing Market Index, 2000–10, monthly data, seasonally adjusted.

After the recession began, job losses in residential construction accelerated, and employment fell by 830,000, or 27 percent, from the start of the recession through June 2009. New home sales, housing starts, and the Housing Market Index also fell further, to record lows. Job losses eventually spread beyond new home construction to other areas of housing as spending on remodeling and home improvement projects fell. As home values declined, homeowners were less willing to invest in home renovation projects because the perceived return on investment and the ability to tap home equity both declined while the value of new loans and leases in bank credit from commercial banks decreased substantially. During the recession, residential construction accounted for over half of the losses in construction as a whole. Residential specialty trade contractors, with losses of 567,000, was the primary driver of job losses within residential construction.

Sensitive to housing's role in the economy, federal policymakers enacted a series of policy initiatives to stabilize the housing market, including tax credits and expanded support for the housing mortgage market. The Housing and Economic Recovery Act of 2008 provided for a tax credit of up to $7,500 for first-time homebuyers. In 2009, the credit was expanded and the deadline was extended for new home purchases.[7] It appears that these acts helped slow residential construction job losses substantially.

As of December 2010, residential construction had yet to recover the jobs lost during the downturn. Losses slowed significantly in the second half of 2009 (by an average of 19,000 jobs per month), and employment edged down in 2010 (by an average of 9,000 jobs per month). A number of other construction indicators also remained at historically low levels in 2010.

LOSSES IN NONRESIDENTIAL CONSTRUCTION

Soon after the recession started, employment losses began in the nonresidential components of construction as well. (See chart 3.) Since an employment trough in November 2003, nonresidential construction—which consists of nonresidential building construction, heavy and civil engineering construction, and nonresidential specialty trade contractors—had added jobs at a rapid pace until the employment level flattened just prior to the recession.

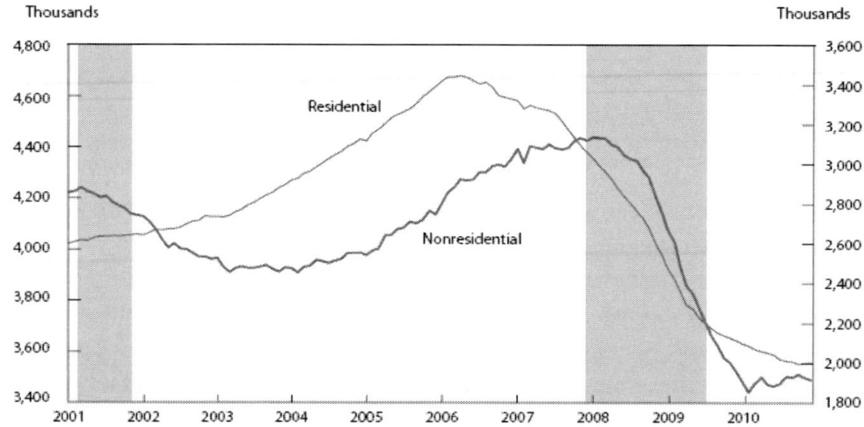

Note: Shaded areas represent recessions as determined by the National Bureau of Economic Research.

Source: U.S. Bureau of Labor Statistics.

Chart 3. Residential and nonresidential construction employment, monthly data, seasonally adjusted, 2001 –10.

Significant job losses began in the second quarter of 2008 and accelerated rapidly; overall, there was a 14.8-percent decrease in employment during the recession. Nonresidential specialty trade contractors was the primary driver of losses within nonresidential construction during the recession, accounting for 377,000 of the 654,000 jobs lost.

Nonresidential construction is highly dependent on the broader economy and government spending. As the economy contracted, there was less demand for offices, factories, and retail facilities; troubles in financial markets also resulted in less funding for new projects. Furthermore, the federal government, state governments, and local governments experienced declining tax revenues, which led to reductions in government spending on civil works projects and affected employment in heavy and civil engineering construction.

In early 2009, the America Recovery and Reinvestment Act of 2009 provided increased spending for infrastructure projects, such as highways and bridges, but even after the recession ended in June 2009, heavy job losses continued in nonresidential construction. The industry lost an additional 330,000 jobs in the 8 months following the end of the recession. Employment has since stabilized and grew by 50,000 between February 2010 and December 2010.

CONSTRUCTION EMPLOYMENT DURING RECESSIONS

Construction is a cyclical industry that tends to go through periodic robust expansions and pronounced contractions. However, even in the volatile history of the construction industry, the 2007–09 recession stands out. Employment losses easily exceeded the declines observed during past recessions. Before 2007–09, the worst employment losses in construction during a recession occurred during the November 1973–March 1975 recession, when employment fell by 604,000. This represented a 14.3-percent drop in construction employment, compared with a 19.8-percent decrease during the 2007–09 recession. The job losses in construction during the latest recession represented 19.8 percent of total nonfarm employment losses.

End Notes

[1] The data on employment used in this article are from the Current Employment Statistics (CES) survey, which is a monthly survey of approximately 140,000 nonfarm businesses and government agencies representing approximately 440,000 individual worksites. For more information on the CES program's methods, see "Technical Notes to Establishment Survey Data Published in Employment and Earnings," http://www.bls.gov/web/cestn2.htm (visited

Apr. 5, 2011). CES data are available at http://www.bls.gov/ces (visited Apr. 5, 2011). The CES data used in this article are seasonally adjusted unless otherwise noted.

[2] Recessions are identified by the National Bureau of Economic Research (NBER). According to the NBER, the most recent recession began in December 2007 and ended in June 2009. The previous two recessions were from March 2001 to November 2001 and from July 1990 to March 1991. For a complete list of business cycle dates, consult the NBER webpage at http://www.nber.org/cycles/cyclesmain.html (visited Nov. 2, 2010).

[3] S&P/Case-Shiller Home Price index data are courtesy of Standard & Poor's and can be found at http://www.standardandpoors.com/indices/sp-case-shiller-home-price-indices/en/us/?indexed=spusaspusacashpidff--p-us---- (visited Apr. 6, 2011).

[4] Data on new home sales are published by the U.S. Census Bureau and are available at http://www.census.gov/const/www/ newressalesindex.html (visited Apr. 6, 2011).

[5] Data on new residential construction (housing starts) are published by the U.S. Census Bureau and are available at http://www.census. gov/const/www/newresconstindex.html (visited Apr. 6, 2011).

[6] Data on the Housing Market Index are published by the National Association of Home Builders and are available at http://www.nahb. org/reference_list.aspx?sectionID= 134 (visited Apr. 6, 2011).

[7] Taxpayers had to have a binding contract to purchase a home before May 1, 2010, and must have closed on the home before July 1, 2010. For more information, see http://www.irs. gov/newsroom/ article/0,,id=204671,00.html (visited Dec. 22, 2010).

In: The Construction Sector in the U.S. Economy ISBN 978-1-61942-893-5
Editors: N. M. McDonald et al.

Chapter 4

THE U.S. HOUSING BUBBLE AND BUST: IMPACTS ON EMPLOYMENT*

Kathryn J. Byun**

Several years ago, conditions in the U.S. economy—such as ease in the credit market—worked to create a prime situation for the first national bubble in U.S. home prices since that which preceded the Great Depression.[1] Generally, housing demand is restrained as prices rise in the market because buyers can no longer qualify for traditional loans. New "affordability" mortgage products considerably relaxed this restraint, thereby allowing the recent boom period to continue much longer than previous expansionary periods. Nontraditional loans were increasingly granted with fewer requirements for buyers to provide documentation to verify that their income could support the mortgage payment.[2] Moreover, these loans were often granted with little or no down payment. Mortgage-backed securities also contributed to the bubble by increasingly financing these high-risk loans throughout the bubble years.

By late 2005, the rapid growth of investment in residential structures had come to an end. Shortly thereafter, other indications of the oncoming bust became visible. First-time home buyers were increasingly priced out of the

---

* This is an edited, reformatted and augmented version of a piece in the Monthly Labor Review, dated December 2010.

** Kathryn J. Byun is an economist in the Division of Industry Employment Projections, Office of Occupational Statistics and Employment Projections, Bureau of Labor Statistics

market, mortgage rates rose by roughly 1 percent, affordability of homes decreased substantially, and speculators pulled out of the market. The market correction has been much more abrupt than the onset of the bubble. Roughly a decade of growth of investment in residential structures was eliminated over just 3 years—from 2005 to 2008. Home prices, as measured by Robert Shiller's real price index, have fallen considerably from their peak in 2006 to levels more consistent with earlier data. Whether or not the bottom of the cycle has been reached is not yet clear, as recent housing data remain relatively mixed.

The recent dynamic housing market cycle has had a considerable impact on the U.S. job market. Input–output (I–O) data published by the BLS Employment Projections Program (EPP) can be used to estimate the number of jobs related to residential construction spending, employment that includes jobs in the construction sector and jobs in all the industries that supply intermediate products and services demanded by residential construction. On the basis of I–O calculations presented later in this article, EPP estimates that demand for residential construction grew from supporting 5.5 million jobs, or 4.2 percent of all U.S. employment, in 1996, to 7.4 million jobs, or 5.1 percent of total employment, at the peak of the cycle in 2005. As the housing market crashed, residential-constructionrelated employment fell substantially; it was at 4.5 million in 2008, accounting for only 3.0 percent of total U.S. jobs.

Not all of the employment growth during the expansionary period is necessarily related to the bubble, as some increases would have been expected with an expanding population and normal economic growth. Given an alternative "nonbubble" demand scenario, I–O analysis allows one to estimate how much of the job growth was due to the bubble as opposed to "normal" economic growth. The estimated alternative demand is necessarily an approximation. The uncertainty of the start date of the recent housing cycle makes determining "nonbubble" demand an even more difficult exercise at this time.

In order to account for the uncertainty of the timing of the bubble's onset, two possible start dates of the housing market bubble are evaluated, 1996 and 2002, allowing for a range of estimated impacts. Two models are considered to estimate nonbubble demand: Because BLS projections do not forecast business cycle activity and instead focus on long-run trends, previously published projections serve as one tool for approximating nonbubble demand, and a naïve constant growth model serves as the second tool. Depending on the start date, the bubble is estimated to have contributed somewhere between 1.2 million and 1.7 million jobs in 2005, accounting for 0.8 percent to 1.2

percent of total U.S. employment. The housing market correction has also had a considerable effect on the U.S. job market. Residential-construction-related jobs are estimated to have been 1.7 million to 2.2 million fewer in 2008 than they would have been had there not been a bubble. According to these estimates and the embedded assumptions, the bust pulled down 2008 U.S. employment by 1.1 percent to 1.5 percent.

In the sections that follow, the housing bubble is analyzed through demand and price data. Construction sector employment data are discussed as inputs into EPP's employment requirements table and as a commonly cited measure of the employment impacts of the housing market. EPP's methods are discussed, and estimates of "residential-construction-related employment" during the recent boom-and-bust cycle are presented. Finally, growth scenarios based on nonbubble demand are considered in order to estimate how the housing boom and bust have affected U.S. employment.

BUBBLE PERIOD

An economic bubble occurs when "trade is in high volumes at prices that are considerably at variance with intrinsic values."[3] The data discussed in this section show unusual growth and falloff in demand for housing and an unprecedented rise and decline in real home prices; behavior indicative of a bubble. Although the rise in demand in the U.S. housing market that occurred through 2005 is now widely referred to as a bubble, when this bubble began is not yet apparent. This is still the subject of much debate and may never be clear, but certainly not until the trough is long past. However, in order to discuss the behavior and impacts of the housing bubble and crash, it is first necessary to come to some decision on when the bubble occurred.

Relying upon input–output analysis, the research presented in this article utilizes the measure of investment in residential structures, as calculated with Bureau of Economic Analysis (BEA) final-demand data, as the metric of the relative size of growth and decline over the housing bubble and bust.[4] The final-demand data show that the climax of the bubble was in 2005, so that year will serve as the endpoint in this analysis. It should be noted, however, that other housing market measures did not peak until 2006, including the price index and industry employment data, examined later.

In the demand data, the bubble's starting point is much less apparent than its endpoint. The expansionary period started in 1991, but when this growth became a bubble is debatable. Many different start dates have been discussed, but years from the late 1990s and early 2000s are the most often suggested. Some people, including Thomas Lawler, an independent analyst who worked for Fannie Mae from 1984 to 2006, contend the bubble started in 2002. Lawler claims that, as the tech-stock bubble came to an end in 2000, investors focused on real estate as an alternative investment vehicle. The low interest rates set by the Federal Reserve over the following few years provided further incentive for home buying. He further asserts that relaxed lending standards helped demand continue when prices reached levels that most people could not otherwise have afforded.[5]

Others contend the bubble began much earlier. For example, Dean Baker, codirector of the Center for Economic and Policy Research, argues the bubble started in 1997. Baker holds that the runup in demand and prices for housing was in large part due to the increased trade deficit and financial market deregulation in the 1990s.[6] Robert Shiller has pointed out that prices, as measured by the Case–Shiller 10-city home price index, rose from 1995 to 2006, and he therefore refers to this as the boom period.[7] As explained earlier, for the purpose of this article, two potential start dates will be examined, allowing for comparisons between a lengthier bubble and a shorter one: 1996, between the onset of the runup in prices and Baker's asserted bubble start date, and 2002, as proposed by Lawler.

MEASURES OF THE BUBBLE AND BUST

Several measures of the bubble and bust are presented here in order to compare data on the magnitude of growth and decline during the bubble and bust years. Although the price data offer important information regarding certain economic effects, residential-construction-related employment over the recent bubble and bust years has more closely tracked measurements related to the demand for homes than the prices paid for the homes. Regardless, I–O analysis dictates that final-demand data be used to gauge the magnitude of the bubble. Other demand-related estimates of housing market activity are presented here as comparative measures of the housing bubble and the bust. The alternative data sources offer measures of the relative size of the bubble and bust that are similar to those in the final-demand data. The similarity in data lends support to the use of final demand as an acceptable metric to gauge the impact of the housing bubble and bust on U.S. employment.

Demand for residential structures

BEA's measure of investment in residential structures comprises construction of single-family and multifamily homes and other residential structures. To calculate the estimate, BEA estimates the value of new construction and then makes adjustments such as adding the value of brokers' commissions on the sale of new and used structures, the value of improvements to structures, and the value of investment in manufactured homes.[8] Theory holds residential investment as a leading economic indicator, as is depicted in chart 1. The gray bars represent recessions as declared by the National Bureau of Economic Research. Residential investment tends to be procyclical, meaning that it generally peaks prior to the onset of recessions and reaches its trough before the end of recessionary periods. BEA estimates demand for residential structures as far back as 1929. In the early years, demand was affected considerably by the Great Depression, falling by nearly 80 percent from 60.0 billion dollars in 1929 to 12.6 billion in 1933.[9] Demand recovered gradually until 1941 and then experienced another dip during World War II followed by a rapid recovery in the latter half of the 1940s.

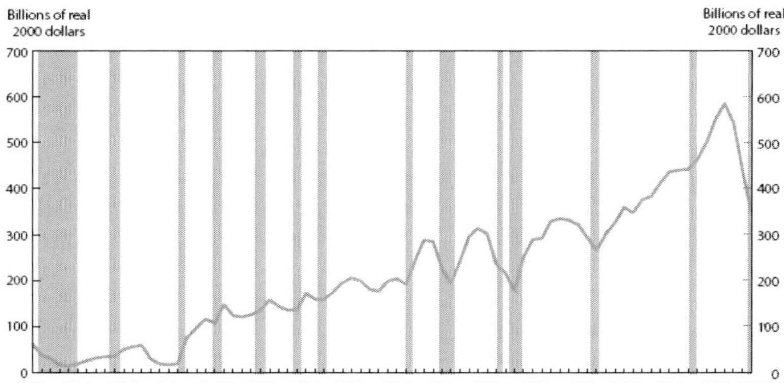

Note: The shaded bars denote National Bureau of Economic Research (NBER)-designated recessions.

Source: Bureau of Economic Analysis (data published June 25, 2009).

Chart 1. Residential investment, 1929–2008.

Growth was somewhat more stable in the 1950s and 1960s, with more moderate declines during economic downturns. Its behavior then became more dynamic starting in the 1970s. Demand experienced peaks followed by troughs around the time of the 1970s oil crises and the energy crisis in 1979. Investment in residential construction once again struggled during the "double-dip recessions" in 1980 and 1982 while buyers faced record-high mortgage rates. As the economy recuperated and interest rates declined, demand recovered until the onset of the savings and loan crisis in the late 1980s. Demand then continued to fall through the recession of 1990–91.

Residential construction then underwent an unprecedented expansionary period that consisted of 14 years of positive growth over 1991–2005, with the exception of a slight decline over 1994–95. Growth in demand over the 1991–2005 period was more than double that of any other expansionary period in the U.S. housing market since 1950. For the first time in the post-World War II era, an expansionary period continued throughout a recession. In fact, some argue that appreciation in home prices stimulated consumer spending and thereby helped to keep the 2001 recession relatively short and shallow.[10] Annual growth rates of demand over this expansionary period were moderate given historical behavior; however, by 2005, 14 years of growth had left demand far above what would be expected given the long-run trend.

Demand more than doubled from 1991 to 2005, from 264.0 billion real dollars to 586.0 billion. Some of this expansion was to be expected as a result of normal cyclical activity. From 1996 (one of the years considered as a starting point for the bubble) to 2005, demand increased by 210.9 billion dollars, with average annual growth of 5.1 percent. More than half of the growth, 123.8 billion, occurred between 2002 and 2005, when demand grew much faster—by 8.2 percent annually. After the bubble period came to an end, in just 3 years demand fell back to 351.3 billion (the 2008 figure), near the 1995 level.

Prices of residential structures

As defined earlier, a bubble arises when demand is high and prices "are considerably at variance with intrinsic values." Therefore, it is not surprising to see that, during the recent housing cycle, prices were affected more than demand. Chart 2 depicts Robert Shiller's real home price index, published in *Irrational Exuberance*,[11] updated with data through 2009. From 1929 through the mid-1940s, as the market suffered through the Great Depression and World War II, the Shiller real home price index stayed close to 60. During the mid-1940s, prices exhibited rapid growth, and the index reached 86.6 in 1947. Prices then remained relatively stable through the late 1990s, with the exception of some cyclical activity in the late 1970s and late 1980s. Outside of the Great Depression and recent bubble period, home prices have closely followed changes to overall prices as measured by the Consumer Price Index. From 1996 to 2006, the Shiller real price index nearly doubled, from 87.0 to 160.6, with 65.7 percent of this growth occurring from 2002 to 2006. Prices quickly plunged thereafter, and the index was at 105.7 in 2009. This surge in growth followed by rapid decline is unprecedented in the history of U.S. real housing prices.

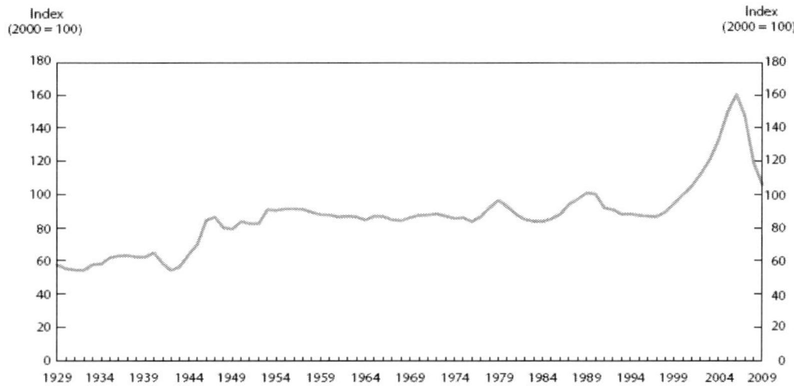

Source: http://irrationalexuberance.com. To view the data, click on the link in the second bullet point on the main Web page.

Chart 2. Robert Shiller real house price index, 1929–2009.

Other measures

There are several demand-related estimates available that could be used as an alternative to the final-demand estimate published by BEA. Data on the value of construction put in place (estimated by the Census Bureau), for example, show a nominal increase from 1996 to 2005, 138.1 percent, similar to that shown by the BEA nominal demand data, 132.1 percent.[12] (See chart 3.) If 2002 is used as the starting point, the two measures show nearly equivalent estimates of percentage growth.

The decline from the peak in 2005 to 2008 was only slightly steeper as measured by the value of construction put in place than as measured by nominal final demand (42.5 percent compared with 37.1 percent, respectively). Since the data on the value of construction put in place are a primary input into

BEA's estimate of final demand, the similarity between the "construction put in place" estimates of growth and decline and the corresponding final demand estimates is to be expected.

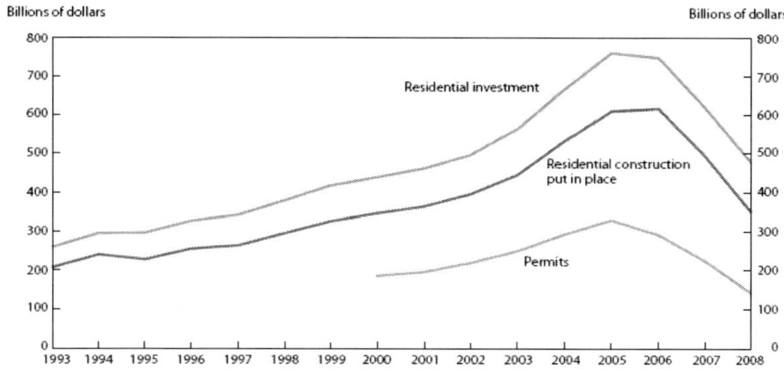

Sources: Bureau of Economic Analysis and Census Bureau.

Chart 3. The nominal value of residential investment, of permits, and of residential construction put in place, 1993–2008.

Data on permits authorized for new privately owned housing units, also published by the Census Bureau, are another measure of housing market activity. Since data for permits are available starting from 2000, only the later bubble start date is examined here. From 2002 to 2005, the number of permits increased by 50.2 percent, similar to the increase in nominal final demand during the same period, which was 53.3 percent. In contrast, there was disparity between the two measures from 2005 to 2008: permits fell by 57.0 percent, and final demand declined by 37.1 percent.

The final measure used for comparison, private housing starts, shows the biggest discrepancy compared with final demand but still exhibits a similar pattern over the bubble-and-bust cycle, as shown in chart 4. Growth in housing starts was 41.1 percent between 1996 and 2005, compared with a 56.2-percent increase in final demand. From 2002 to 2005, the two measures show closer estimates of growth. Housing starts declined by 56.6 percent from 2005 to 2008 while demand declined by 40.1 percent.

The rate of growth during the housing boom is very similar across the four measures. The decline from 2005 to 2008 was slightly less dramatic in the demand data than in the other estimates. It may be that demand data lag the other data and would track more closely overall if the 2009 measures were available.[13] Because of the nature of I–O models, the research presented later in this article necessarily relies on final-demand data to measure the impact of the housing bubble on U.S. employment. Analysis shows only relatively minor discrepancies in measurement of growth and decline between the final-demand data and the other demand-related measures.

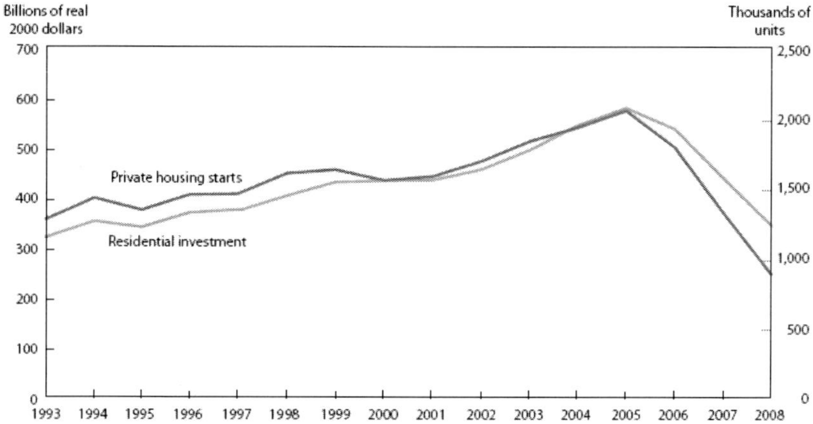

Source: Bureau of Economic Analysis.

Chart 4. Annual residential investment (left axis) and annual private housing starts (right axis), 1993–2008.

Employment Trends in Construction

To gauge the impact of the housing bubble on the job market, researchers often look to BLS estimates of employment within the construction sector. BLS publishes two such measures of employment, the Current Employment Statistics (CES) estimate and the Current Population Survey (CPS) estimate.[14] The CES survey is an establishment, or payroll, survey that estimates only wage and salary employment, whereas the CPS is a household-based survey that also captures unpaid family workers and the self-employed. The CES survey counts jobs, while the CPS counts persons. In assembling its projections, the EPP is interested in a total jobs count, analyzing trends in wage and salary employment as well as the employment of unpaid family workers and the self-employed. EPP takes the slightly unconventional step of summing CES data for wage and salary workers with the CPS estimate of self-employed and unpaid family workers to arrive at an estimate of total jobs. In doing so, EPP implicitly assumes within its industry employment data that each self-employed or unpaid family worker counted by the CPS has only one job.[15]

EPP estimates of total employment within the construction sector are presented in chart 5.[16] The total employment measure is available only for the aggregate construction sector, which comprises residential building construction, nonresidential building construction, heavy and civil engineering construction, and specialty trade contractors. During the recent housing cycle, employment in the construction sector peaked in 2006, 1 year after the demand climax. Because employment data for the construction sector are available through 2009, they are included in this discussion even though data on final demand are available only through 2008. Also, since employment peaked 1 year later in the employment data than in the demand data, this allows for a comparison of 3 years of decline in each of the time series.

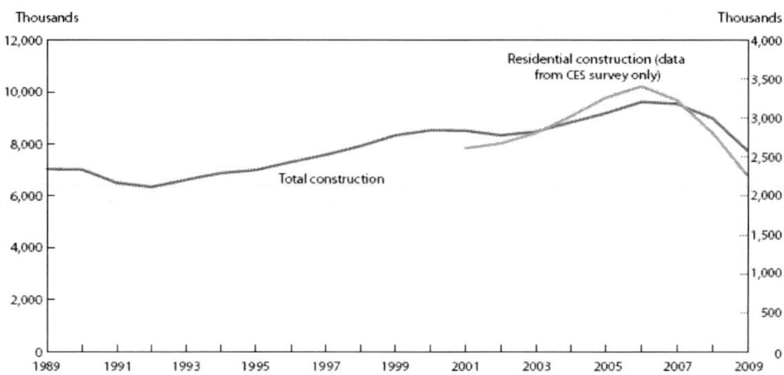

Sources: Total construction employment is measured as the the sum of wage and salary employment from the Current Employment Statistics survey and the number of self-employed workers and unpaid family workers from the Current Population Survey. The line showing employment in residential construction exhibits data from the Current Employment Statistics survey only.

Chart 5. Total employment in the construction sector (left axis) and employment in residential construction (right axis), 1989–2009.

Employment in the construction sector grew notably, by 2.3 million jobs, or 31.6 percent, between 1996 and 2006. More than half of this growth, 1.3 million jobs, occurred from 2002 to 2006. From 2006 to 2009, employment fell by 1.9 million jobs, a decline of 19.4 percent. These data indicate that the housing bubble and bust had a considerable impact on U.S. construction employment, but it is important to bear in mind that they cover employment in the construction sector as a whole, not just in residential construction.

A measure of residential construction employment alone is of course preferable for isolating the impacts of the housing bubble and bust on residential construction. Unfortunately, with regard to data on unpaid family workers and the self-employed, the CPS does not break out the construction sector into more detailed components. The CES survey disaggregates construction employment into the following: construction of buildings (residential and nonresidential), heavy and civil engineering construction, and specialty trade contractors (residential and nonresidential). However, specialty trade contractors has been broken out only since 2001. Summing residential building construction and residential specialty trade contractors data results in what this article refers to as data on "residential construction."[18] Summing the CES data shows that residential construction employment made up between 37.6 percent and 44.5 percent all employment in the construction sector from 2001 to 2009. During the same period, nonresidential construction accounted for 42.6 percent to 48.4 percent of construction sector employment, and heavy and civil engineering construction supplied 12.8 percent to 14.0 percent.

Residential construction showed faster employment growth during the bubble and steeper decline over the bust period than the construction sector as a whole. From 2002 to 2006, employment in residential construction increased by 26.6 percent, considerably faster than the 15.4-percent growth in the construction sector as a whole. Of the 1.3 million jobs added in construction, more than half—715,000—were in residential construction. From 2006 to 2009, wage and salary employment within residential construction industries declined by 1.1 million, or 33.4 percent, while the total number of construction jobs fell by 1.9 million, or 19.4 percent.

The effects of the housing bubble and bust were not limited to the construction sector. Record sales of existing and new homes during the housing boom propelled economic growth throughout the economy. Though the impact of the housing boom cannot directly be seen in every industry within CES data, some industries appear to rely heavily on demand for residential construction, including those shown in italics in table 1.[17] Employment in cement and concrete product manufacturing and in construction machinery manufacturing grew by 5.1 percent and 9.0 percent, respectively, from 2001 to 2006 while overall employment in manufacturing fell by 13.9 percent.[18] Employment in the real estate credit industry and the mortgage and nonmortgage loan brokers industry ballooned by 52.0 percent and 119.5 percent, respectively. The housing boom appears to have supported job growth not only in these industries, but also in the industry group of offices of real estate agents and brokers and that of activities related to real estate.

As the housing bubble deflated and the United States entered a recession, industries that heavily depend on demand from residential construction began to suffer considerable losses in employment, losses much greater in percentage terms than those sustained in the overall economy. Employment in real estate credit and in mortgage and nonmortgage loan brokers fell back to 2001 levels or even lower by 2009. Wood product manufacturing and cement and concrete product manufacturing also suffered extensive losses in employment from 2006 to 2009, much greater than the average loss across all manufacturing sectors.

Table 1. Current Employment Statistics estimates of employment in select industries, in thousands, select years, 2001–09

Industry	2001	2006	2009	Numerical change		Percentchange	
				2001–06	2006–09	2001–06	2006–09
Totalnon-farm	131,826.0	136,086.0	130,920.0	4,260.0	–5,166.0	3.2	–3.8
Total private	110,708.0	114,113.0	108,371.0	3,405.0	–5,742.0	3.1	–5.0
Construc-tion	6,826.0	7,691.0	6,037.0	865.0	–1,654.0	12.7	–21.5
Construc-tion of buildings	1,588.9	1,804.9	1,365.6	216.0	–439.3	13.6	–24.3
Residential buildings	781.4	1,008.8	639.4	227.4	–369.4	29.1	–36.6
Non-residen-tial buildings	807.5	796.1	726.2	-11.4	–69.9	–1.4	–8.8
Heavy and civil engineering	953.0	985.1	846.9	32.1	–138.2	3.4	–14.0
Specialty trade	4,283.9	4,901.1	3,824.4	617.2	–1,076.7	14.4	–22.0
Residential specialty trade contractors	1,848.1	2,396.8	1,629.6	548.7	–767.2	29.7	–32.0
Non-residential specialty trade contractors	2,435.8	2,504.4	2,194.9	68.6	–309.5	2.8	–12.4
Manufact-uring	16,441.0	14,155.0	11,883.0	– 2,286.0	–2,272.0	–13.9	–16.1
Wood products	574.1	558.8	360.7	–15.3	–198.1	–2.7	–35.5
Cement and concrete products	236.2	248.3	187.7	12.1	–60.6	5.1	–24.4

Industry	2001	2006	2009	Numerical change		Percentchange	
				2001–06	2006–09	2001–06	2006–09
Architectural and structural metals	421.8	411.6	348.3	–10.2	–63.3	–2.4	–15.4
Construction machinery	71.3	77.7	67.4	6.4	–10.3	9.0	–13.3
Wholesale trade	5,772.7	5,904.5	5,625.3	131.8	–279.2	2.3	–4.7
Lumber and construc-tion supply	220.5	264.1	205.1	43.6	–59.0	19.8	–22.3
Retail trade	15,238.6	15,353.3	14,527.8	114.7	–825.5	0.8	–5.4
Furniture stores	281.8	298.9	224.3	17.1	–74.6	6.1	–25.0
Building material and garden supply stores	1,151.8	1,324.1	1,162.6	172.3	–161.5	15.0	–12.2
Financial-activities	7,808.0	8,328.0	7,758.0	520.0	–570.0	6.7	–6.8
Real estate credit	231.2	351.4	196.9	120.2	–154.5	52.0	–44.0
Mortgage and non-mortgage loan brokers	66.0	144.9	66.0	78.9	–78.9	119.5	–54.5
Real estate	1,343.4	1,499.0	1,416.7	155.6	–82.3	11.6	–5.5
Offices of real estate agents and brokers	291.1	374.6	305.2	83.5	–69.4	28.7	–18.5
Activities related to real estate	437.6	521.9	537.2	84.3	15.3	19.3	2.9

RESIDENTIAL-CONSTRUCTION-RELATED EMPLOYMENT

By combining the total jobs estimate with other output measures, EPP assembles a time series of historical input–output tables.[19] I–O tables provide detailed information on the flows of goods and services that make up the production processes of U.S. industries. The employment requirements table, one table within the National Income and Product Accounts, measures the number of jobs supported through the entire production process.[20] The table estimates the thousands of jobs required by each industry to satisfy a million dollars of final demand for a given good or service.

The employment requirements table illustrates what is driving industry employment with respect to both final demand and to the production of intermediate goods and services, applying an input–output view to industry data. Exhibit 1 depicts the employment requirements table in a simplified three-industry economy: manufacturing, construction, and all other industries. The entries in each row show direct and indirect employment in each industry. Direct employment, shown in the upper left, middle, and bottom right of the table, measures the employment within the producing industry necessary to generate the primary good or service produced by the given industry. Indirect employment, represented by all cells in the matrix other than those along this diagonal, is the employment generated in all of the industries that support the producing industry with their inputs.[21] For example, I_{mc} represents the indirect employment in the construction sector supported by demand for manufacturing goods.

Employment requirements table

	Manufacturing	Construction	Other		Vector of final demand
Manufacturing	D_m	I_{cm}	I_{om}		FD_m
Construction	I_{mc}	D_c	I_{oc}	$\times$	FD_c
Other	I_{mo}	I_{co}	D_o		FD_o

Total employment = direct employment + indirect employment

Direct employment =

Manufacturing	$D_m \times FD_m$
Construction	$D_c \times FD_c$
Other	$D_o \times FD_o$

Indirect employment =

Manufacturing	$(I_{cm} \times FD_c) + (I_{om} \times FD_o)$
Construction	$(I_{mc} \times FD_m) + (I_{oc} \times FD_o)$
Other	$(I_{mo} \times FD_m) + (I_{co} \times FD_c)$

NOTE: D = direct employment, I = indirect employment, FD = final demand, m = manufacturing, c = construction, and o = other

Exhibit 1. Analysis of a simplified employment requirements table.

As residential construction boomed, secondary effects spilled over into many industries generating indirect employment (since building new homes required purchases of intermediate goods and services). Employment in the manufacturing sector, for example, benefited because of purchases of intermediate goods such as carpet, toilets, countertops, and construction equipment that went into the construction of new homes or improvements on existing structures. Even seemingly unrelated industries, such as legal services, benefited indirectly from surging demand for residential construction. As the money spent on construction projects increased, construction companies probably required more legal support.

Multiplying a given row of the employment requirements table, say, construction, by the vector of total final demand calculates the number of jobs within the sector. In 2005, for example, the CES survey estimated 7.3 million wage and salary jobs in the construction sector and the CPS reported 1.8 million self-employed workers and unpaid family workers, resulting in an EPP estimate of 9.2 million total jobs in the construction sector. Multiplying the construction row of the employment requirements table by EPP's vector of total final demand shows that 8.2 million of the jobs within the construction sector were attributable to direct employment. That is, these jobs satisfied demand for goods classified in the construction sector. The remaining 1.0 million indirect jobs added to final demand for other goods and services by providing construction activity as an input. For example, when consumers paid their hospital bills, some of that money went to pay employees in the construction industry who did work for the hospitals. EPP estimates that 59,000 jobs in the construction sector supplied work that served as an intermediate input into the hospitals industry.

THE 2008–18 EMPLOYMENT PROJECTIONS

Although this article is focused on the recent impacts of the housing bubble and bust, EPP's 2008–18 projections are briefly discussed as they relate to the housing market. EPP expects that construction will be the only sector among goods-producing sectors to show employment growth over the projected period.[1]

Construction was more heavily affected by the 2007–09 recession than other goods-producing sectors and is therefore expected to show higher growth in the recovery period.

EPP anticipates demand for residential construction to recover to 581.6 billion dollars in 2018, very near the peak level of 586.0 billion in 2005. The projected level of demand is expected to support 6.2 million residentialconstruction-related jobs in 2018, near the 2003 level but not as high as the level in 2004 or 2005. EPP expects that residential-construction-related employment will climb back to 3.8 percent of total employment in 2018, higher than the 3.0 percent level of 2008 but lower than the 5.1 percent level of 2005 and slightly lower than the 1993 level. Sixty percent of the residential-constructionrelated jobs lost between 2005 and 2008, or 1.7 million, are anticipated to be recovered over the projection period.

[1] For more information on industry employment projections, see Rose Woods, "Industry output and employment projections to 2018," Monthly Labor Review, November 2009, pp. 52–81.

Rather than looking at a particular row within the employment requirements table to break out sector employment by what types of demand the industry in question is satisfying, one can analyze the table in its entirety to estimate how demand results in employment in all industries throughout the U.S. job market. Multiplying the employment requirements matrix in its entirety by the column vector of final demand for investment in residential construction yields an estimate of what this article refers to as "residential-construction-related employment." EPP's analysis of direct and indirect employment includes data only for the construction sector as a whole. Determining employment impacts related specifically to demand for residential construction requires the assumption that the relationship of jobs to demand is the same for residential as for aggregate construction.

Because investment in residential construction requires purchases of many intermediate goods and services from a variety of industries, the effects of the housing bubble spread throughout the economy. Construction output attributable to residential construction spending grew from 695.3 billion dollars in 1996, to 827.0 billion in 2002, to slightly over 1.0 trillion dollars in 2005. The purchases of intermediate goods and services for residential structures accounted for nearly half of this output. During the bust period, output related to residential construction demand fell, and it was at 600.2 billion in 2008.[22]

EPP estimates that output related to residential construction spending led to employment of 5.5 million in 1996. As the housing market expanded, related employment grew to 6.0 million jobs in 2002. By the peak of the housing market, in 2005, it had increased to 7.4 million. Employment expanded by 1.8 million jobs, or by 33.4 percent, between 1996 and 2005, with 1.4 million of this growth occurring between 2002 and 2005. As the bubble burst, residential-construction-related employment fell to 4.5 million in 2008, 385,000 fewer jobs than in 1993, the earliest year of available data.

Residential construction spending supported an estimated 4.0 percent to 4.4 percent of total employment within the United States from 1993 to 2000. By 2005, employment related to residential construction reached 5.1 percent of total U.S. employment; it then fell, reaching 3.0 percent in 2008. (See chart 6.) Since it makes up only a small portion of total employment, residential-construction-related employment usually has not had a considerable impact on overall employment change in the U.S. economy. It is interesting to note that, according to EPP's estimates, in 2008 the decline in residential-construction-related employment—1.2 million—was greater than the overall net loss in employment in the U.S. economy—804,000.

EMPLOYMENT GROWTH ATTRIBUTABLE TO THE BUBBLE

Not all of the residential-construction-related employment growth during the bubble period was generated from the housing bubble, given that some increases would have been expected for reasons including population growth and continued expansion in the economy. I–O tables allow researchers to conduct an in-depth analysis of the economy-wide effects that a change in final demand has on industry output as well as employment.[23] By estimating what demand would have been without a bubble, one can measure how many U.S. jobs there would have been under the alternative demand scenario. The difference between the actual number of jobs and the number approximated under the scenario of nonbubble demand serves as an estimate of the number of jobs due to the housing bubble.

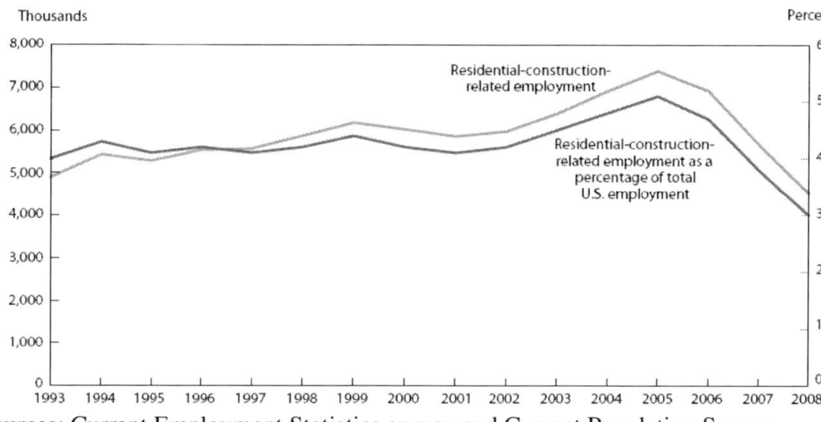

Sources: Current Employment Statistics survey and Current Population Survey.

Chart 6. Residential-construction-related employment in thousands (left axis) and as a percentage of total U.S. employment (right axis), 1993–2008.

This type of analysis is necessarily uncertain and relies upon a number of assumptions. The alternative demand scenarios are only approximations, as no one knows what would have happened without a housing bubble. The bubble had reverberating impacts throughout the economy that are impossible to isolate from other economic activity. Relying upon I–O tables for impact analysis also requires assumptions. For example, I–O accounts are defined such that each industry has a unique production function. It is assumed that there are no economies of scale in production. In addition, changes in final demand are assumed to be achieved instantaneously and without price changes.

Given that the 10-year projections of employment and macroeconomic activity that EPP publishes every 2 years are not a forecast, previous EPP projections provide one estimate of investment in residential construction without a bubble. Predicting shocks over 10 years is usually impossible. Moreover, in spite of economic shocks, the economy tends to revert to long-run trends. Therefore, BLS projections are not a forecast of business-cycle activity.[24]

Accounting for both 1996 and 2002 as possible start dates for the bubble, the 1996–2006 and 2002–12 projections serve in this article as one method of estimating nonbubble demand for residential structures. BLS publishes a point projection for a 10-year period, so it does not publish data for intervening years. Because of large- scale revisions, data published in previous projections are not comparable to more recently published data, but the projected growth rate usually is comparable. Therefore, the projected average annual growth rate is applied to actual demand data from the proposed start date of the bubble. A naïve model of constant growth is also considered, wherein the average annual growth rate from 1950 to 1996 or from 1950 to 2002 continues to hold throughout the bubble period.

Nonbubble demand scenarios

The 1996–2006 projections were prepared using the Standard & Poor's DRI (Data Resources, Inc.) U.S. quarterly model.[25] At the time of that publication, BLS expected demographics to be the main factor changing the growth in demand for residential construction over the projected decade. An expected decline in the number of people in the age groups typically thought of as those of first-time home buyers was anticipated to hold growth to 0.8 percent annually over the projection period, in comparison with the 2.1 percent exhibited on average annually between 1950 and 1996. If the bubble did start in 1996 and the projections accurately captured demand without the bubble, 86.0 percent of growth in demand for residential structures between 1996 and 2005, or 181.4 billion dollars, was attributable to the housing market bubble. In another scenario, if growth had continued at the 1950–96 average annual pace, the bubble contributed an estimated 134.9 billion dollars of investment, 64.0 percent of growth, over the 1996–2006 period. (See chart 7.)

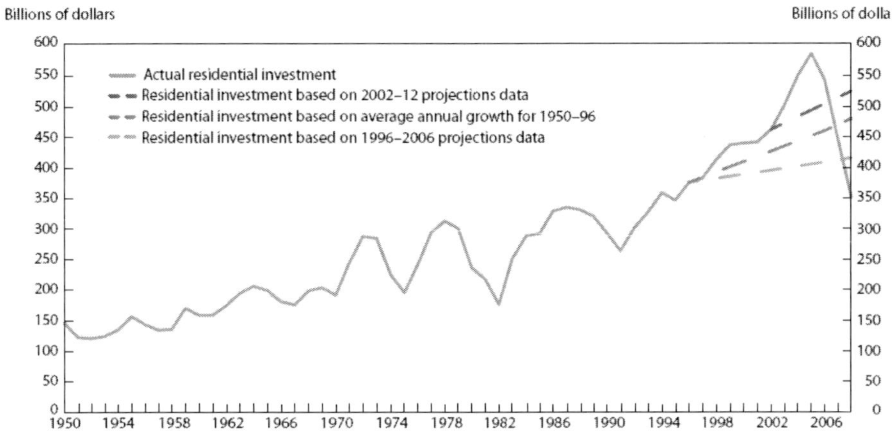

Sources: Bureau of Economic Analysis and Bureau of Labor Statistics.

Chart 7. Nominal residential investment from 1950 to 2008 and hypothetical "nonbubble" demand estimated for 1996–2008 and for 2002–08.

The 2002–12 projections were prepared by use of the macroeconomic model developed by Macroeconomic Advisers, LLC.[26] EPP once again stated that demographics were expected to slow investment in residential structures. However, rapid growth during the late 1990s and early 2000s likely contributed to a projected annual growth rate of 2.1 percent from 2002 to 2012, higher than the rate projected for 1996–2006. The average annual growth rate from 1950 to 2002 was 2.2 percent, nearly equivalent to the 2002–12 projection. Because results based on the naïve constant growth model for 1950–2002 are nearly identical to those based on the 2002–12 projections, the constant growth model for 1950–2002 is not examined separately. If the bubble started in 2002, demand for residential construction in 2005 was 93.3 billion dollars higher than nonbubble demand as measured by the 2002–12 projections. According to this model, three quarters of the growth exhibited from 2002 to 2005 was attributable to the bubble.

From 2005 to 2008, demand for residential structures fell considerably as the market corrected for rapid growth during the boom years. In 2008, demand was only slightly higher than its 1995 level. All of the proposed models anticipated that demand for residential construction would be higher than it was in 2008. If the bubble began in 1996, on the basis of the 1996–2006 projections, demand would be expected to be 18.1 percent higher in 2008 than it actually was. On the basis of average annual growth from 1950 to 1996, growth would be expected to be 36.6 percent higher than it actually was. If the bubble started in 2002, demand would be projected to be 49.5 percent higher than it actually was.

Related nonbubble employment

The alternative demand estimates were combined with data from the employment requirements table to estimate the impacts of the bubble and bust throughout the U.S. job market. (See chart 8.) On the basis of the 2002–12 projections, the number of residential-construction-related jobs was approximated to be 1.2 million over the theoretical nonbubble level at the peak of the housing market in 2005. According to this estimate, 82.7 percent of the job growth between 2002 and 2005 was a result of the housing bubble. Also, the bubble is estimated to have increased U.S. employment by 0.8 percent in 2005.

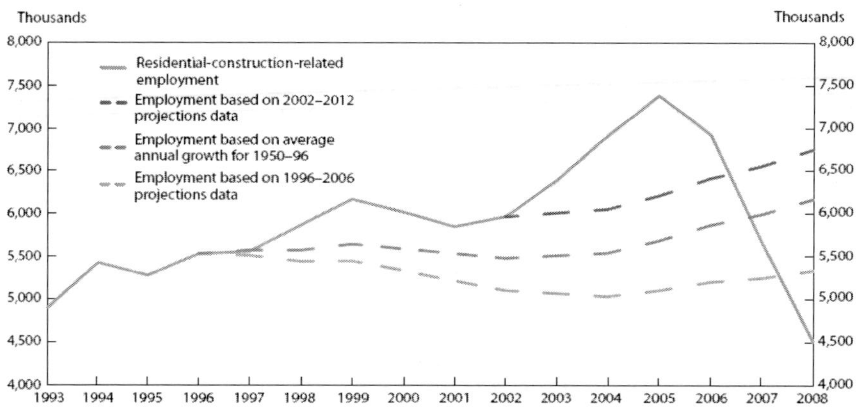

Chart 8. Residential-construction-related employment from 1993 to 2008 and hypothetical "nonbubble" employment estimated for 1996–2008 and 2002–08.

If, however, the bubble started in 1996, the constant growth model implies that employment was 1.7 million over nonbubble residential-construction-related employment and contributed 1.2 percent to the total number of U.S. jobs in 2005. According to the 1996–2006 projections, employment was to stay relatively flat between 1996 and 2008, with a slight dip in the between years. In this nonbubble scenario, residential-construction-related employment was expected to fall by 433,000 between 1996 and 2005.

The decline in nonbubble employment present in the 1996–2006 projections could be due to a number of factors. The assumptions underlying I–O analysis may be having some impact here. For example, the production function may not have been the same without a bubble. Perhaps output was higher in relation to employment in the construction industry during the bubble than it would have been without a bubble. Alternatively, the projections could have underestimated nonbubble demand. Regardless, because nonbubble residential-construction-related employment was expected to decline from 1996 to 2006, the results of this model are disregarded because they are considered to be too low.

By 2008, housing-related employment fell to 4.5 million and was accounting for only 3.0 percent of total U.S. jobs. If the bubble began in 1996, the naïve growth model expects that, if the market were not correcting for excess growth in the bubble years, residential-construction-related employment would have been 1.7 million higher in 2008. If the bubble did not begin until 2002, it is approximated that residential construction-related employment would have been 2.2 million higher in 2008. The bust in the housing market, according to these measures and the embedded assumptions, pulled down U.S. employment by 1.1 percent to 1.5 percent below where it would have been had there not been a bubble.

In recent years, the housing boom and bust have had a substantial impact on the U.S. job market. Because the date of the onset of the bubble is not clear, this article considers two possible starting points, 1996 and 2002. Whereas industry employment data offer analysis of employment within the entire construction sector, I–O data published by EPP can be used to estimate the level of employment related to a specific category of demand and related purchases of intermediate goods and services. In this article, residential-construction-related employment was analyzed. Stimulated by the bubble in the housing market, demand for residential construction grew by 56.2 percent from 1996 to 2005, with much of this growth occurring during the last 3 years. Given EPP's assumptions, its data imply that the growth in demand for residential construction accounted for an increase of 1.8 million jobs from 1996 to 2005, of which 1.4 million appeared from 2002 to 2005. Because of the burst of the bubble, residential-construction-related employment fell by 2.9 million from 2005 to 2008.

Some of the growth in employment related to residential construction was to be expected because of normal economic expansion, whereas some was propelled solely by the housing bubble. Two types of models—one a naïve constant growth model and the other based on previous BLS projections—

were evaluated to estimate what the level of investment in residential structures would have been without the bubble stimulating growth. The 1996–2006 projections and the average annual growth model for 1950–1996 were compared to estimate the employment impacts of the bubble with the assumption that it started in 1996. The projections implied that, had there not been a bubble, residential-construction-related employment would have declined slightly over the bubble period; therefore, this estimate was considered too low. The constant growth model was thus considered the preferable measure for the earlier start date of the bubble. Because the constant growth model for 1950–2002 and the 2002- to-2012 projections were nearly equivalent with regard to employment related to residential construction, only the projections were examined for the later start date.

The constant growth model projected only 153,000 of the 1.8 million rise in residential-construction-related employment from 1996 to 2005. The model indicates that, by 2005 (the peak of the bubble), the housing bubble supported 1.7 million jobs, or 1.2 percent of total U.S. employment. The BLS 2002–12 projections indicate that, if the bubble started in 2002, residential-construction-related employment would have grown by 244,000 from 2002 to 2005 without a bubble, as compared with the job growth of 1.4 million jobs that actually occurred. According to this model, residential-construction-related employment was 1.2 million jobs over the nonbubble level and accounted for 0.8 percent of U.S. employment in 2005.

The decline over 2005 to 2008 was much more abrupt than the growth that had recently occurred, and it nearly matched the growth exhibited over 1993 to 2005. EPP data show that residential-construction-related employment fell from 7.4 million jobs in 2005 to 4.5 million in 2008, which was 385,000 fewer than existed in 1993. Depending on the bubble start date, employment is estimated to have been between 1.7 million and 2.2 million below nonbubble employment in 2008. According to these estimates and the embedded assumptions, the bust in the housing market pulled down 2008 U.S. employment to 1.1 percent to 1.5 percent lower than where it would have been had there not been a bubble.

End Notes

[1] For more discussion on comparisons of the current bubble-andbust cycle in home prices to that of the Great Depression, see David C. Wheelock, "The Federal Response to Home Mortgage Distress: Lessons from the Great Depression," the Federal Reserve Bank of St.

Louis *Review*, May/June 2008, pp. 133–48, on the Internet at http://research.stlouisfed.org/publications/review/08/05/Wheelock.pdf (visited July 14, 2010).

[2] See Shayna M. Olesiuk and Kathy R. Kalser, "The Sand States: Anatomy of a Perfect Housing-Market Storm," on the Internet at www.fdic.gov/bank/analytical/quarterly/2009_vol3_1/AnatomyPerfectHousing.html (visited Dec. 1, 2010).

[3] Ronald R. King, Vernon L. Smith, Arlington W. Williams, and Mark V. van Boening, "The Robustness of Bubbles and Crashes in Experimental Stock Markets," in Richard H. Day and Ping Chen, eds., *Nonlinear Dynamics and Evolutionary Economics* (New York, Oxford University Press).

[4] "Residential investment" and "final demand for residential structures" are used interchangeably in this article.

[5] See James R. Hagerty, "Who's to Blame for the Housing Bubble?" *The Wall Street Journal,* WSJ Blogs, Nov. 16, 2009, on the Internet at http://blogs.wsj.com/developments/2009/11/16/whos-to-blamefor-the-housing-bubble/ (visited Dec. 1, 2010).

[6] See Dean Baker, "East Asia's economic revenge," *guardian. co. uk*, on the Internet at www.guardian.co.uk/commentisfree/cifamerica/2009/mar/09/usa-useconomy (visited Apr. 10, 2010).

[7] See Robert J. Shiller, "Don't Bet the Farm on the Housing Recovery," *New York Times*, Apr. 10, 2010, on the Internet at www.nytimes.com/2010/04/11/business/economy/11view.html?emc=eta1 (visited Dec. 1, 2010).

[8] For a more thorough discussion of BEA's data on private structures, see Paul R. Lally, "How BEA Accounts for Investment in Private Structures," *Survey of Current Business* (U.S. Department of Commerce, Bureau of Economic Analysis, February 2009), pp. 9–15, on the Internet at www.bea.gov/scb/pdf/2009/02%20February/0209_ briefing_structures.pdf.

[9] All dollar figures in this article, unless otherwise noted, are real values in year-2000 dollars. All BEA data in this article are consistent with figures published as of July of 2009 and with EPP's 2008–18 projections presented in this article.

[10] See Frank E. Nothaft, "The Contribution of Home Value Appreciation to US Economic Growth," *Urban Policy and Research,* March 2004, pp. 23–34, on the Internet at www.freddiemac.com/news/pdf/ contribution_homevalue.pdf; and Kevin B. Moore and Michael G. Palumbo, *The Finances of American Households in the Past Three Recessions: Evidence from the Survey of Consumer Finances* (Washington, DC, Federal Reserve Board, Dec. 10, 2009), on the Internet at www.federalreserve.gov/pubs/feds/2010/201006/ 201006pap.pdf (visited Dec. 1, 2010).

[11] Several other price indices are often cited when referencing the housing market, including the Case–Shiller 10 and 20, the Case– Shiller national, and the Federal Housing Finance Agency house price index, but these indexes have historical data going back no further than 1987. Note that, for the years 1987–2009, the Shiller real index is based on the Case–Shiller national index adjusted by the Consumer Price Index measurement of inflation. Earlier years are based on other price measures. For further information on the Shiller real index, see Robert J. Shiller, *Irrational Exuberance,* second edition (Princeton University Press, 2005); see also http://irrationalexuberance.com/ (visited Mar. 22, 2010).

[12] Data on construction put in place and data on permits are not adjusted for changes in prices and are therefore compared with the nominal final-demand data published by BEA.

[13] BEA implemented a comprehensive revision to its National Income and Product Accounts in July of 2009. The estimates for 2009 are not comparable with earlier annual data as published by EPP because they were based upon BEA data as published before the comprehensive revision.

[14] There are many differences between CPS and CES data, only a few of which are mentioned here. For a comparison between the two surveys, see www.bls.gov/bls/empsitquickguide.htm (visited July 19, 2010).

[15] That is, EPP assumes that the count of self-employed and unpaid family workers is the equivalent of a jobs count. CPS data are also used by EPP to estimate wage and salary

employment in industries for which the CES survey does not provide estimates, including the agricultural and private household industries.

[16] The CPS program estimated data for 1983–2002 on the basis of the old Standard Industrial Classification (SIC) codes. Data for 2000–09 are based on the North American Industry Classification System (NAICS). (For 2000–02, data were calculated both within the framework of NAICS and within that of the SIC system.) The 1983–99 data were adjusted to account for the coding change.

[17] The industries in table 1 were selected on the basis of those included in Matthew Miller, "A visual essay: post-recessionary employment growth related to the housing market," *Monthly Labor Review*, October 2006, pp. 23–34.

[18] Wood product manufacturing and architectural and structural metals manufacturing did see slight declines in employment over 2001–06. However, these declines were minor in comparison with the loss of jobs in the overall manufacturing sector. Also, both showed much larger declines over 2006–09 than over 2001–06, suggesting that the housing bubble may have held onto jobs that otherwise would have been lost during this period.

[19] BEA's benchmark I–O accounts provide the most comprehensive picture available of transactions within the U.S. economy, but are published only once every 5 years. The 2002 benchmark I–O data, released in 2007, were the latest data available for EPP's 2018 projections. On the basis of the 2002 benchmark I–O data, annual data from the National Income and Product Accounts, annual Census data, and data from a host of other sources, EPP estimates a historical time series of I–O data, currently 1993 to 2008. For detailed information regarding the 2002 benchmark I–O accounts, see Ricky L. Stewart, Jessica Brede Stone, and Mary L. Streitwieser, "U.S. Benchmark Input-Output Accounts, 2002," *Survey of Current Business* (U.S. Department of Commerce, Bureau of Economic Analysis, October 2007), pp. 19–48. For a more complete discussion of the methods used by EPP, see the *BLS Handbook of Methods*, chapter 13, on the Internet at www.bls.gov/ opub/hom/ homch13_a.htm (visited Apr. 5, 2010).

[20] The employment requirements table is "import adjusted"; that is, it is modified to account only for the sales of domestically produced goods and services to final users because imported goods generally do not generate domestic employment.

[21] All employees, direct and indirect, earn income that will generally be spent on consumer goods and services, which, in turn, will generate a third type of employment called induced employment (also referred to as "income multiplier effects on employment"). The Bureau of Labor Statistics does not measure induced employment.

[22] Estimating total output related to a specific category of final demand requires the assumption that the employment requirements table estimated for the economy as a whole also holds at the more detailed level.

[23] See Mary L. Streitwieser, "A Primer on BEA's Industry Accounts" (U.S. Department of Commerce, Bureau of Economic Analysis, June 2009), on the Internet at www.bea.gov/scb/ pdf/2009/06%20June/0609_indyaccts_primer_a.pdf (visited Dec. 6, 2010).

[24] The projections do, however, include in-house projections of the growth of the population, an important contributor to growth within the housing market. For more discussion on how BLS's assumptions affected the 1996 to 2006 projections, see Ian Wyatt, "Evaluating the 1996–2006 employment projections," *Monthly Labor Review,* October 2010, pp. 33–69.

[25] For more information on the 1996–2006 projections, see Thomas Boustead, "The U.S. economy to 2006," *Monthly Labor Review,* November 1997, pp. 6–22.

[26] For more information on the 2002–12 projections, see Betty W. Su, "The U.S. economy to 2012: signs of growth," *Monthly Labor Review,* February 2004, pp. 23–36.

In: The Construction Sector in the U.S. Economy ISBN 978-1-61942-893-5
Editors: N. M. McDonald et al.

Chapter 5

COMPENSATION OF RESIDENTIAL AND NONRESIDENTIAL CONSTRUCTION WORKERS*

Thomas Moehrle

For more than two decades, the Employer Cost for Employee Compensation (ECEC) publications available from the U.S. Bureau of Labor Statistics have reported estimates of the mean hourly costs for wages and benefits tabulated across industries, occupations, and labor force characteristics. The data for these estimates are drawn from the National Compensation Survey (NCS).[1] What makes ECEC statistics particularly useful for data users is the comprehensive detail of cost-level estimates for compensation components such as paid leave, health insurance, and contributions to retirement plans. Although the ECEC tabulations (published quarterly) currently serve a broad set of data users, the expansion over the last several years in the size of the NCS samples, along with enhancements in the industry classification system, have provided opportunities to examine—through the use of industry averages—industries that were once veiled from standard statistical analysis. This article presents compensation estimates for subsets of the construction sector, estimates that allow for an examination of recent

* This is an edited, reformatted and augmented version of an Office of Compensation and Working Conditions at the Bureau of Labor Statistics publication, dated April, 2010.

trends in wages and benefits of workers employed in residential and nonresidential construction activities.

Standard ECEC publications provide data on compensation in the overall construction sector, but a more detailed analysis of subsectors, industry groups, and industries shows that compensation patterns for the construction sector as a whole mask important differences within the sector. The industry analysis in this article shows that workers in nonresidential construction typically earn more than workers in residential construction in the same subsector and that, for the construction of buildings subsector, the differential grew from 2004 to 2009.

CLASSIFICATION IN THE CONSTRUCTION SECTOR

As all other BLS establishment surveys do, the NCS classifies surveyed establishments according to the North American Industry Classification System (NAICS)—the industry classification standard adopted by the United States, Canada, and Mexico—which classifies establishments into sectors. Every sector has a two-digit code. Within each sector, establishments are further grouped into subsectors (three digits), industry groups (four digits), and industries (five digits). Through the first five digits, NAICS codes are comparable across the United States, Canada, and Mexico. A sixth digit is used for further detail within any of the three countries.[2] Three subsectors are defined for construction: construction of buildings (NAICS 236), heavy and civil engineering construction (NAICS 237), and specialty trade contractors (NAICS 238). Heavy and civil engineering construction entails projects such as highway and dam construction, which at best indirectly relate to residential and nonresidential construction projects. Because this study focuses on residential and nonresidential construction workers, establishments classified under heavy and civil engineering construction are excluded. To further refine the analysis, only establishments within the private sector are studied. Table 1 displays some of the NAICS codes in the construction sector.

The establishments classified under construction of buildings are involved principally in the construction of residential and commercial buildings, or the remodeling and maintenance of existing buildings. Many of these establishments are general contractors, operative builders, or remodelers who may contract part or all of the production work of a given construction project. Construction of buildings is divided into two industry groups: residential building construction (NA-ICS 2361) and nonresidential building construction

(NAICS 2362). This grouping conveniently facilitates comparisons within the subsector. Although NAICS has been officially used in the United States only since 1997, its predecessor—the Standard Industry Classification (SIC) system—organized the categories within construction of buildings in much the same way; the close similarities provide the continuity necessary to construct, at least in part, a historical economic perspective of residential and nonresidential trends.[3] The perspective is incomplete, however, because the construction of buildings subsector covers less than 25 percent of total construction employment.

Approximately 63 percent of all construction jobs are located in the specialty trade contractors subsector. Unlike the industry groups and industries within construction of buildings, those within the subsector of specialty trade contractors are defined by the types of production tasks carried out— such as carpentry, framing, electrical work, and plumbing— and not by whether activities are residential or nonresidential. Although the standard NAICS design does not distinguish residential construction from nonresidential construction in the specialty trade contractors subsector, BLS has used the last digit of the NAICS code to distinguish between these two activities.[4] The NAICS codes that BLS has added appear under the specialty trade contractor subsector in table 1.[5]

Table 1. BLS NAICS code summary for the construction sector, March 2009

Title	Classification	NAICS code	Percent ofemployment[1]
Construction	Sector	23	100.0
Construction of buildings	Subsector	236	22.9
Residential building	Industry		
construction	group	2361	10.7
Nonresidential	Industry		
building construction	group	2362	12.2
Heavy and civil engineering	Subsector	237	13.6
Specialty trade contractors	Subsector	238	63.5
Residential specialty	Industry		
trade contractors	(BLS)	238001	26.7
Nonresidential specialty	Industry		
trade contractors	(BLS)	238002	36.8

[1] The data used to calculate the estimates in this column are not seasonally adjusted.

To gather a sense of the relative importance of residential and nonresidential activities, the article discusses employment trends for residential and nonresidential construction in the subsectors of specialty trade contractors and construction of buildings before turning to compensation patterns. The employment data in the article come from the Current Employment Statistics (CES) program at BLS. These data are not seasonally adjusted.

EMPLOYMENT TRENDS

Chart 1 shows employment trends in construction of buildings, and chart 2 shows employment trends for specialty trade contractors.[6] Because of the continuity of building construction data from SIC to NAICS, the charted data for that subsector stretch back to 1990, whereas the specialty trade contractors series is mapped back only to 2001. The data in the charts reveal that, although the two subsectors have very different employment levels, the patterns from 2001 and later are directionally similar. Residential construction employment in both subsectors increased with the residential housing boom in the early years of the decade until it began to contract in 2006, whereas nonresidential employment in both subsectors fell as the effects of the 2001 recession rippled through the economy and then climbed until 2008 when employment levels throughout the economy again began to contract.

Employment trends in construction of buildings

In a 2006 Monthly Labor Review article,[7] John Mullins studied trends in residential and nonresidential construction employment. Using the building construction data series, Mullins reported that until the end of the 1990s employment trends of residential establishments and nonresidential establishments followed similar paths, although the latter had a larger share of employment. Establishments in both industries shed large numbers of people from payrolls in the first few years of the 1990s and then experienced relatively steady employment growth through the remaining years of that decade. (See chart 1.)

Although the patterns of residential and nonresidential construction were similar through the 1990s, there are notable differences, most notably that employment in residential construction dropped more sharply in the early years and grew more rapidly in the later years. The quicker paced job growth pushed the level of residential employment past that of nonresidential employment during 1999.

The similarities that had appeared in the 1990s dissipated by the new century. With the exception of a moderate decline from March 2000 to April 2001, establishments in residential building construction continued to add workers to payrolls—at an unprecedented rate—until the early part of 2006. Notably, the short and shallow recession of 2001 that stretched from March to November of that year appears not to have had any long-term ill effects on employment in residential building construction. The same cannot be said of nonresidential construction, however.

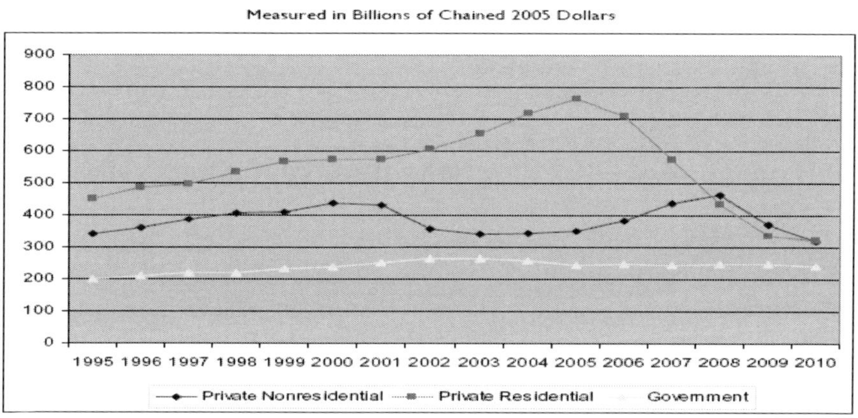

Chart 1. Employment in residential and nonresidential construction of buildings, private industry, seasonally adjusted, January 1990–July 2009.

After adding jobs from 1993 through 1999, establishments in nonresidential building construction curtailed job creation as employment flattened in 2000 before precipitously falling through most of the period from 2001 through 2003. The divergent trends of the two industry groups resulted in an unparalleled widening of employment levels: residential construction employment grew by more than 10 percent between 2001 and 2004, and non-residential construction employment decreased by more than 10 percent during that same period. When residential employment peaked in early 2006, it exceeded nonresidential employment by 223,000, a marked difference from what had occurred in the 1990s.

Mullins links this sudden divergence in employment paths to a confluence of events. He points out that the nonresidential construction industry was clearly affected by the recession of 2001—which was characterized by businesses cutting back on investment spending, while the residential side of the market shrugged off any recessionary drag. In fact, the residential housing market actually accelerated during the same period, as several socioeconomic factors—including historically low interest rates— came together. Among the factors Mullins cites are the growth in baby boomers' demand for second homes and their children's desire to purchase their first homes.

Since Mullins' 2006 article, employment in residential building construction has plummeted by nearly a third, falling from its April 2006 peak of 1.0 million to under 690,000 in July 2009. Employment in nonresidential establishments also has fallen, but not as steeply. Nonresidential employment peaked at 844,000 in March 2008 before falling and eventually hitting 726,000 in July 2009, a 14-percent decline. To date, it appears that both industry groups continue the downward trend.

Employment trends in the specialty trade contractors subsector

The specialty trade contractors subsector has exhibited patterns remarkably similar to those of the construction of buildings subsector. Together, charts 1 and 2 show that employment in residential construction experienced nearly the same periods of growth and contraction in the two subsectors, as did employment in nonresidential construction. What is clearly different between the two subsectors is the level of employment: as of July 2009, employment in specialty trade contractors was 2.8 times larger than employment in building construction, making the former the predominant subsector of construction.

In specialty trade, nonresidential employment exceeded residential employment by nearly 650,000 in January 2001 (2.5 million compared with 1.8 million), but the extraordinary growth in residential employment brought the two employment levels together by early 2006, the period in which residential employment in the subsector peaked. Residential employment in the subsector grew by about 34 percent during the 5-year period to peak at over 2.4 million.

Similar to what happened in building construction, employment in nonresidential establishments of specialty trade contractors fell with the 2001 recession to a low of 2.3 million before expanding from March 2003 to January 2008, when it peaked at 2.6 million. Both industries have shed jobs since their peaks. According to CES estimates, residential employment fell by 30 percent from its peak to 1.7 million as of July 2009, and nonresidential employment fell 16 percent from its peak to 2.2 million as of July 2009. In percentage terms, the comparable industries in both subsectors experienced very similar employment declines from their respective peaks.

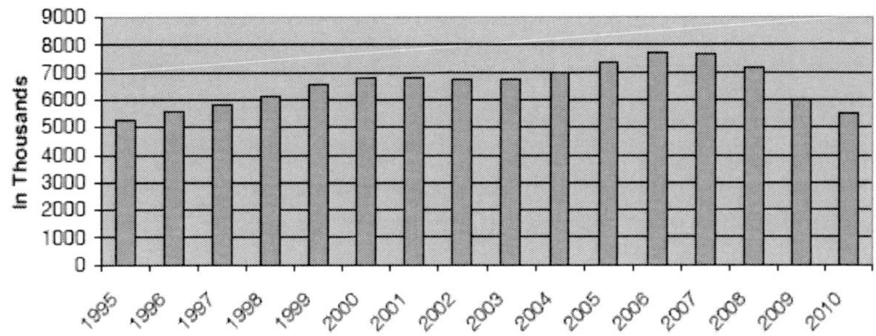

Chart 2. Employment among specialty trade contractors involved in residential and nonresidential construction, private industry, seasonally adjusted, January 2001–July 2009.

Certainly, trends in employment can have effects on compensation levels. To capture these effects within particular industries, ECEC cost-level estimates are calculated through the use of sample weights calibrated to the level of industry employment at the time of the survey.

For this study, sample weights are calibrated to account for changes in employment among the construction subsectors—inclusive of shifts among the residential and nonresidential industries—by use of employment data from the CES program. When sample weights are adjusted to mirror employment trends at the time of the survey, aggregated compensation data—such as estimates for all residential workers or all nonresidential workers—will move more in accordance with employment. The next section of the article discusses these compensation estimates.

COMPENSATION PATTERNS

In March 2004, the NCS program made a major transition regarding how ECEC compensation data are tabulated and published by industry and occupation. A switch was made from publishing industry estimates under the SIC system to publishing them under NAICS. The classification of occupations also was changed, from the occupational classification system of the 1990 Census of the Population to the 2000 Standard Occupational Classification

(SOC) system.[8] As an extension of the ECEC tabulations by industry, table 2 presents estimates of employer costs for employee compensation by residential and nonresidential construction activities for the construction of buildings subsector, and table 3 does the same for the specialty trade contractors subsector.[9]

Although ECEC publications provide estimates for March, June, September, and December of each year, the tables presented in this article contain only March estimates but span the years from 2004 through 2009, the only years for which ECEC estimates are available under NAICS.[10] Tables A-1 and A-2 of the appendix provide the relevant relative standard errors, which measure the statistical reliability of these estimates.

Table 2. Mean employer costs for employee compensation per hour worked and costs as a percent of total compensation in the construction of buildings subsector (NAICS 236), private industry, March data, 2004–09

Item	March 2004		March 2005		March 2006	
	Residential	Non-residential	Residential	Non-residential	Residential	Non-residential
Employment (in thousands)[1]	844.4	703.3	911.3	716.3	987.1	763.4
	Costs per hour worked					
Total compensation	$26.61	$30.84	$28.06	$32.22	$26.80	$34.83
Wages and salaries	19.59	22.09	19.72	22.90	19.28	23.91
Total benefits	7.02	8.74	8.34	9.33	7.52	10.92
Paid leave	.98	1.37	1.00	1.45	.97	1.60
Supplemental pay	.95	.85	1.61	1.00	1.41	1.28
Insurance	1.19	1.81	1.57	1.97	1.46	2.54
Health	1.15	1.70	1.52	1.86	1.41	2.39
Retirement and savings	.73	1.32	.78	1.48	0.60	1.77
Legally required[2]	3.18	3.39	3.38	3.41	3.07	3.73
	Percent of total compensation					
Total compensation	100.0	100.0	100.0	100.0	100.0	100.0
Wages and salaries	73.6	71.6	70.3	71.1	71.9	68.6
Total benefits	26.4	28.4	29.7	28.9	28.1	31.4
Paid leave	3.7	4.4	3.6	4.5	3.6	4.6
Supplemental pay	3.6	2.8	5.7	3.1	5.3	3.7
Insurance	4.5	5.9	5.6	6.1	5.4	7.3
Health	4.3	5.5	5.4	5.8	5.3	6.9
Retirement and savings	2.7	4.3	2.8	4.6	2.2	5.1
Legally required[2]	11.9	11.0	12.1	10.6	11.5	10.7

Item	March 2007		March 2008		March 2009	
	Residential	Non-residential	Residential	Non-residential	Residential	Non-residential
Employment (in thousands)	942.1	797.4	832.9	817.8	638.0	725.9
	Costs per hour worked					
Total compensation	$26.69	$35.65	$26.25	$38.32	$27.18	$41.12
Wages and salaries	19.64	24.15	19.81	26.15	20.23	28.06
Total benefits	7.06	11.50	6.44	12.17	6.94	13.06
Paid leave	.98	1.50	.91	1.59	1.06	1.87
Supplemental pay	1.47	1.32	1.09	1.23	1.13	1.19
Insurance	1.25	2.79	1.10	2.90	1.28	3.15
Health	1.21	2.62	1.06	2.71	1.23	2.96
Retirement and savings	.39	2.06	.38	2.34	.41	2.43
Legally required[2]	2.97	3.83	2.97	4.11	3.07	4.42
	Percent of total compensation					
Total compensation	100.0	100.0	100.0	100.0	100.0	100.0
Wages and salaries	73.6	67.7	75.5	68.2	74.5	68.2
Total benefits	26.4	32.3	24.5	31.8	25.5	31.8
Paid leave	3.7	4.2	3.5	4.2	3.9	4.5
Supplemental pay	5.5	3.7	4.1	3.2	4.2	2.9
Insurance	4.7	7.8	4.2	7.6	4.7	7.7
Health	4.5	7.3	4.0	7.1	4.5	7.2
Retirement and savings	1.5	5.8	1.4	6.1	1.5	5.9
Legally required[2]	11.1	10.8	11.3	10.7	11.3	10.8

[1] The data in this row are not seasonally adjusted.

[2] Those benefits which are legally required are OASDI, Medicare, Federal and State unemployment insurance, and workers' compensation.

The estimates reveal interesting differences in compensation structure between residential and nonresidential construction. For most of the years reported in tables 2 and 3, residential workers earned less in total compensation than nonresidential workers. Tables A-3 and A-4 of the appendix present differences in hourly compensation—by component of compensation—along with the t-statistics of each of these differences. The *t*-statistics presented in the tables gauge the statistical significance of the estimated differences in compensation. When one is interpreting the statistical significance of a difference presented in this article, a *t*-statistic greater than 1.65 is associated with statistical significance at the 90-percent level of confidence. Most differences for total compensation, wages and salaries, and total benefits are statistically significant, particularly for the years from 2006 forward. All compensation figures in this article are nominal.

Table 3. Mean employer costs for employee compensation per hour worked and costs as a percent of total compensation in the specialty trade contractors subsector (NAICS 238), private industry, March data, 2004–09

Item	March 2004		March 2005			March 2006
	Residential	Non-residential	Residential	Non-residential	Residential	Non-residential
Employment (in thousands)[1]	1,987.8	2,197.7	2,136.7	2,231.9	2,322.6	2,365.4
	Costs per hour worked					
Total compensation	$21.01	$29.96	$21.72	$30.20	$22.68	$30.97
Wages and salaries	15.58	20.34	15.90	20.46	16.58	20.77
Total benefits	5.43	9.62	5.83	9.74	6.10	10.20
Paid leave	.55	1.06	.59	1.01	.66	1.20
Supplemental pay	.64	.87	.65	.80	.61	.95
Insurance	.99	2.31	1.09	2.41	1.34	2.58
Health	.94	2.25	1.04	2.33	1.28	2.46
Retirement and savings	.47	1.99	0.56	2.07	.66	1.98
Legally required[2]	2.78	3.37	2.94	3.44	2.83	3.49
	Percent of total compensation					
Total compensation.	100.0	100.0	100.0	100.0	100.0	100.0
	Percent of total compensation					
Wages and salaries	74.2	67.9	73.2	67.7	73.1	67.1
Total benefits	25.8	32.1	26.8	32.3	26.9	32.9
Paid leave	2.6	3.5	2.7	3.3	2.9	3.9
Supplemental pay	3.1	2.9	3.0	2.6	2.7	3.1
Insurance	4.7	7.7	5.0	8.0	5.9	8.3
Health	4.5	7.5	4.8	7.7	5.6	7.9
Retirement and savings	2.2	6.7	2.6	6.9	2.9	6.4
Legally required[2]	13.2	11.3	13.5	11.4	12.5	11.3

[1] The data in this row are not seasonally adjusted.

[2] Those benefits which are legally required are OASDI, Medicare, Federal and State unemployment insurance, and workers'compensation.

Compensation patterns in construction of buildings

The differentials in compensation between residential and nonresidential workers within building construction are somewhat varied. In March 2004, residential workers earned a mean of $26.61 per hour in total compensation while nonresidential workers earned a mean of $30.84 per hour in total compensation (table 2), 16 percent more than residential workers. By March 2009, nonresidential construction work paid, on average, 51 percent more in total compensation than residential construction work: total compensation of residential workers was virtually unchanged through the 6-year period while total compensation of nonresidential workers increased to $41.12, a remarkable occurrence given the employment trends of the two industries. Arguably, nominal compensation could be expected to remain relatively flat for residential workers in light of the contraction in employment by a third from April 2006 to July 2009, but the weakening demand for nonresidential workers—evidenced by the 14-percent contraction in that industry group's employment—has not prevented the compensation levels of those workers from rising.

This suggests that the two labor markets— that of residential construction and that of nonresidential construction—are different and should be analyzed separately as well as together.

As did the gap in total compensation, the wage and salary gap widened between 2004 and 2009. In March 2004, the mean of the wages and salaries paid to nonresidential workers was $22.09 per hour, which was not significantly different from residential workers' mean wage, $19.59. But by March 2009, nonresidential workers' average wages had grown to $28.06 and residential wages averaged $20.23—virtually unchanged from 2004. In addition, the estimated difference in wage and salary between residential and nonresidential building construction workers is statistically significant for each of the years from 2006 forward, suggesting fundamental differences in compensation structures emerging over the last few years.[11] Not only are the differences for the later years statistically significant, they are also economically significant. Because the wages paid to residential workers remained virtually flat, real wages—that is, wages adjusted for changes in the Consumer Price Index—fell in residential building construction as the Consumer Price Index increased 13.5 percent between March 2004 and March 2009. Nonresidential workers' wages stayed well ahead of price increases, rising a nominal 27 percent.

Not surprisingly, the wage differences are mirrored in the benefits component of compensation. Employers' costs for the benefits of residential building construction workers were virtually unchanged between 2004 ($7.02 per hour) and 2009 ($6.94 per hour). During that same period, the nonresidential side of the subsector reported benefit costs of $8.74 in 2004 and $13.06 in 2009. Using 2004 as a base and comparing that year with 2009 reveals that the benefit gap expanded from 24.5 percent in 2004 to 88.2 percent in 2009. Part of the divergence in benefit costs resulted from the difference in wage growth. For many workers, the majority of benefit costs are formulaically related to wage levels. For instance, as wages increase, so do the costs of Medicare and Social Security contributions, paid leave, and some supplemental components of compensation such as premium pay for overtime. With wage growth so different between residential and nonresidential building construction workers, a wedge between benefit costs can be expected to emerge naturally. But this is only part of the story. Much of the expansion of the gap in benefit costs can be traced directly to the cost of health insurance and that of retirement and savings, two benefits that are only weakly related to wage levels.

As frequently reported in the news media, health insurance costs have increased substantially over the years. Measured across all private industry workers, Employment Cost Index estimates indicate that employers' costs for health insurance have increased about 30 percent since 2004.[12] However, according to the ECEC estimates of this study, employers' costs for health insurance have remained virtually unchanged for residential workers in building construction, but have increased 74 percent for nonresidential workers in the same subsector. In 2009, employers' health insurance costs were $1.23 per hour for residential workers and $2.96 per hour for nonresidential workers. The mean for all private industry workers was $2 in March 2009.

The cause of the large differences in health insurance costs as measured by ECEC can only be speculated upon. Naturally, more generous health insurance plans drive up costs, as does an increase in the rate of participation in health benefits. However, offsetting these factors are new requirements for some employees who participate in employer provided health plans, requirements such as dollar contributions to accompany employers' contributions. Whether the quality of health-care coverage is better and whether worker participation is higher among nonresidential workers are questions that cannot be answered definitively with ECEC data alone.[13] Nevertheless, with such a large difference in health insurance costs paid by employers, it seems clear that, overall, nonresidential building construction workers have fared better than their counterparts over the last few years in regard to health benefits.

The gap between residential and nonresidential building construction widened even further for retirement and saving benefits.

Between 2004 and 2009, retirement contribution costs decreased by 43 percent for employers in residential building construction whereas they increased 85 percent for employers in nonresidential building construction. Retirement and savings costs include both the costs of defined benefit plans and those of defined contribution plans. In March 2009, retirement costs were $0.41 for residential building construction and $2.43 for nonresidential building construction.[14] The average for all of private industry was $0.96.

Compensation patterns for specialty trade contractors

The gap in total compensation is large and significant in the specialty trade contractors subsector as well, but that differential has been comparatively more stable over the years than that of building construction. In March 2004 in the specialty trade contractors subsector, the mean total compensation of nonresidential construction workers was $8.94 greater than that of residential construction workers; in March 2009 the difference was $8.78.[15] The differences are statistically significant for March of every year from 2004 to 2009. The relatively stable difference in compensation from 2004 to 2009 reflects, in part, similar growth in compensation for the two sets of workers (residential and nonresidential), which stands in contrast to what occurred in building construction. Although the overall gap in compensation between residential workers and nonresidential workers in the two relevant subsectors of construction confirms differences between the markets for residential and nonresidential construction labor, the difference in growth in compensation between residential workers in construction of buildings and those working for specialty trade contractors suggests differences between these two groups of workers as well. The difference in growth in compensation between residential and nonresidential workers in specialty trade appears not to have been affected by the subsector's changing gap in employment, whereas the difference in compensation between residential and nonresidential building construction workers does appear to have been affected by that subsector's changing employment gap.

In the specialty trade contractors subsector, the gap in cost between residential and nonresidential workers is divided nearly equally (in dollar terms) between wages and salaries and total benefits. In March 2009, nonresidential workers were paid mean hourly wages of $22.83 (table 3), $4.17 more than residential workers, and received benefits costing an average of $11.15, $4.61 more than their counterparts.

FACTORS INFLUENCING DIFFERENCES IN COMPENSATION

Differences in compensation between comparable industries can come about from any number of factors. For instance, within a given occupation, it could be the case that nonresidential establishments employ a larger proportion of higher skilled workers than residential establishments. Moreover, the occupational distributions of residential and nonresidential construction work may be very different; for example, it could be that nonresidential establishments employ a greater proportion of people in higher wage occupations—such as managers or engineers—thereby pulling up the average compensation of the industry. And, of course, industry and occupational mix may vary by area of the country, and compensation levels can fluctuate significantly by area of the country.

Regression analysis

Because of the small size of the ECEC subsample of the NCS, for this article's calculations of average compensation by industry, no attempt is made to control for occupational staffing differences among establishments and industries.

However, regression analysis provides a means by which occupational, geographic, and other differences among industries can be statistically controlled while one measures differences in compensation among industries. To model the difference in compensation between the two industries in question, the ECEC microdata were used in a log-linear regression model of compensation levels. The compensation differential of the two industries within each of the two subsectors was isolated by controlling for the occupational mix, the geographical area, and selected occupational characteristics, which were unionization, establishment size, and the number of hours scheduled for work.[16] The regression results show a difference in total compensation between residential and nonresidential construction in the range of 5 percent to 11 percent, a range that is much smaller than the ranges between the industry averages presented in tables 2 and 3; this smaller range suggests that differences in compensation structure between the two sets of workers are not as large as the simple sample-weighted industry averages suggest, but the results of the model do confirm a significant difference in compensation.[17]

OES data

When one controls for occupational distribution and other factors associated with compensation, the ECEC sample cannot support simple sample-weighted industry averages that are statistically reliable (because of the small sample size); however, the Occupational Employment Statistics (OES) program's sample can do so in part. The OES program conducts a large area-based national wage survey for which it canvasses all areas of the country. The national sample consists of 1.2 million establishments from which information is collected over 3 consecutive years. Because of the sample size of the OES survey, wage estimates often can be constructed for the most detailed level of occupations within given industries, and thus users of OES survey data can sometimes compare the average wage of an occupation within a given subsector, industry group, or industry with the same occupation's average wage in a different subsector, industry group, or industry.[18]

The OES program reports residential and nonresidential construction data for only the construction of buildings subsector, but that set of estimates is sufficient to demonstrate that gaps in compensation between residential and nonresidential construction remain across individual occupations. For May 2008, OES reported on 19 major occupational groups within construction of buildings. Not surprisingly, the largest major occupational group in terms of employment was construction and extraction, which accounted for nearly 64 percent of employment in the construction of buildings subsector. For construction and extraction, wages were notably different between residential and nonresidential construction. Workers within residential construction earned an average wage of $19.36 per hour while nonresidential workers earned $22.24 on average, a 15-percent difference. In fact, for the May 2008 results, all but two of the major occupational groups that were compared showed nonresidential workers earning more on an hourly basis than their counterparts.[19]

Still, because major occupational groups are composites of many individual occupations, an analysis of residential and nonresidential construction activity within the groups will of course tell a different story than an analysis of the two industries within individual occupations. Since the major group construction and extraction accounts for the largest percent of employment in the construction sector, it is illustrative to compare detailed occupations within this group. OES data show that carpenters make up the largest percentage of employment within this major group, with 47.8 percent of their employment within the residential industry and 30.6 percent of it within the nonresidential industry. Even within this narrowly defined occupation, wages are notably higher for nonresidential workers. Carpenters in residential construction earned, on average, $19.71 per hour in wages in May 2008, while those in nonresidential construction earned $22.95, a 16-percent difference.[20]

ESTABLISHMENT AND OCCUPATIONAL CHARACTERISTICS

Differences in characteristics of workers, of establishments, and so forth are of interest to many ECEC data users because there are typically correlations between some of the characteristics and compensation levels.[21] Because of the small size of the ECEC sample, employer cost data that are tabulated by any of the characteristics, such as union membership or establishment size, cannot be precisely estimated for the two industries of residential and nonresidential construction, so they are not provided in this study.[22] However, the percentage distributions of these characteristics provide insight into differences among the four sets of workers (residential and nonresidential workers in construction of buildings and at specialty trade contractors) that may result in disparities in compensation. Table 4 shows, for March 2004 and March 2009, the percentage of workers in unions and the percentage with a full-time work schedule, as well as the distribution of workers among four establishment size classes.[23]

Table 4. Percentages for selected characteristics, construction of buildings (NAICS 236) and specialty trade contractors (NAICS 238), private industry, March 2004 and March 2009

Subsector, industry group, or industry	Union		Full time		Establishment size classes (number of workers)							
					1–49		50–99		100–499		500 or more	
	2004	2009	2004	2009	2004	2009	2004	2009	2004	2009	2004	2009
Construction of buildings												
Residential	7.1	2.6	93.6	88.3	88.3	81.6	5.3	8.2	6.4	9.2	.0	1.0
Nonresidential	17.4	22.5	99.5	95.7	56.9	43.1	10.1	23.0	25.3	23.2	7.7	10.7
Specialty trade contractors												
Residential	9.2	9.4	97.4	93.2	76.7	83.0	11.6	8.7	9.8	6.8	1.9	1.5
Nonresidential	33.9	35.0	97.7	97.6	53.5	53.2	14.6	22.1	27.6	21.5	4.2	3.2

For specialty trade contractors, the gap in total compensation has been more stable, undulating only slightly across the 6-year period. In March 2004, total compensation in nonresidential construction was about 43 percent more than that in residential construction. For March 2009, the gap is estimated at about 35 percent. The relative stability in the gap in compensation is attributable to increases in compensation that were only slightly different.

Typically, unionization is correlated with higher levels of compensation, and the compensation estimates in this study are consistent with that correlation.[24] The table shows that in March 2009 nonresidential workers—in both subsectors—had higher incidences of unionization than residential workers. Within building construction, less than 3 percent of residential workers were union members, while nearly 23 percent of nonresidential workers were members. For specialty trade, nearly 10 percent of residential workers were members of unions, whereas 35 percent of nonresidential workers were members. According to data from the Current Population Survey, union membership for the United States was 12.4 percent in 2008.[25]

The distribution of workers according to size of establishment also is revealing. Most construction jobs are found within establishments employing fewer than 100 workers. In March 2009, around 90 percent of workers in residential construction—in both subsectors—worked in establishments with fewer than 100 workers, and approximately 90 percent of these workers (in both subsectors) were employed in establishments with fewer than 50 workers. Less than 2 percent of residential workers were employed in establishments employing 500 or more workers. The distribution of nonresidential workers according to size of establishment is less skewed. In March 2009, about two-thirds of nonresidential construction workers employed in construction of buildings worked at establishments having fewer than 100 workers, and nearly 11 percent of nonresidential building construction workers worked at establishments having 500 or more workers. About 75 percent of specialty-trade nonresidential workers were employed within establishments having fewer than 100 workers; 3 percent were employed at establishments having 500 or more workers. Without regard to the full set of factors influencing levels of compensation, workers in large establishments tend to earn higher wages and salaries and typically have more generous benefit packages.

Compensation of construction workers varies greatly. Estimates derived from the March 2009 NCS survey data show that, in the construction of buildings subsector, the average total compensation of nonresidential workers was 51 percent higher than that of residential workers, and the differences in employer costs were large for both wages and benefits. A smaller gap is present in the specialty trade contractors subsector, in which nonresidential workers earn nearly 35 percent more in total compensation than residential workers. These differences stem from numerous factors, including occupational mix, geographical area, and many occupational characteristics.

For building construction workers, the gap in total compensation between residential and nonresidential workers has widened greatly since 2004, when nonresidential workers received 16 percent more in total compensation. The widening of the gap occurred as nonresidential workers saw hefty increases in compensation while residential workers had virtually unchanged compensation across the 6-year period. Among nonresidential building construction workers, total benefits were up 49 percent from March 2004 to March 2009, increasing substantially faster than wages, which rose by 27 percent. Most of the group's increases in benefits were driven by growth in the amounts employers paid for health insurance (74 percent) and retirement and savings (85 percent) benefits.

APPENDIX: TABLES A-1 THROUGH A-4

Table A-1. Relative standard errors, construction of buildings (NAICS 236), private industry, March data, 2004–09

Item	March 2004		March 2005		March 2006	
	Residential	Non-residential	Residential	Non-residential	Residential	Non-residential
Total compensation	4.2	6.2	3.6	4.2	3.5	3.5
Wages and salaries	3.4	5.0	3.0	3.7	2.8	2.7
Total benefits	7.6	9.1	6.3	5.5	6.0	5.2
Paid leave	14.2	9.5	12.0	7.8	8.5	6.3
Supplemental pay	11.9	11.6	9.6	8.6	9.9	9.3
Insurance	14.7	14.4	11.2	7.7	10.5	6.5
Health	15.1	14.6	11.5	7.7	10.7	6.5
Retirement and savings	23.1	15.2	20.0	13.0	17.4	15.3
Legally required[1]	4.6	6.7	4.8	4.0	4.6	3.6
Item	March 2007		March 2008		March 2009	
	Residential	Non-residential	Residential	Non-residential	Residential	Non-residential
Total compensation	2.3	3.3	2.6	3.5	2.5	3.6
Wages and salaries	1.9	2.6	2.1	2.6	2.2	2.8
Total benefits	4.5	4.9	4.9	5.8	4.8	5.4
Paid leave	8.2	9.5	8.7	8.8	7.2	9.3

Item	March 2007		March 2008		March 2009	
	Residential	Non-residential	Residential	Non-residential	Residential	Non-residential
Supplemental pay	7.6	8.1	8.1	6.9	7.2	9.1
Insurance	9.0	6.9	9.7	8.0	9.7	7.0
Health	8.9	6.9	9.6	7.8	9.6	7.0
Retirement and savings	14.4	11.2	16.4	14.3	17.6	10.4
Legally required[1]	4.3	3.5	4.3	3.9	3.3	3.7

[1] Those benefits which are legally required are OASDI, Medicare, Federal and State unemployment insurance, and workers' compensation.

Table A-2. Relative standard errors for selected characteristics, private industry, construction specialty trade (NAICS 238), March data, 2004–09

Item	March 2004		March 2005		March 2006	
	Residential	Non-residential	Residential	Non-residential	Residential	Non-residential
Total compensation	4.	6.2	3.6	4.2	3.5	3.4
Wages and salaries	2	5.0	3.0	3.7	2.8	2.7
Total benefits	3.4	9.1	6.3	5.5	6.0	5.2
Paid leave	7.6	9.5	12	7.8	8.5	6.3
Supplemental pay	14	11	0	8.6	9.9	9.3
Insurance	2	6	9.6	7.7	10	6.5
Health	11	14	11	7.7	5	6.5
Retirement and savings	9	4	2	13.0	10	15
Legally required[1]	14	14	11	4.0	7	3
Item	March 2007		March 2008		March 2009	
	Residential	Non-residential	Residential	Non-residential	Residential	Non-residential
Total compensation	2.3	3.3	2	3.5	2.5	3
Wages and salaries	1.9	2.6	6	2.6	2.2	6
Total benefits	4.5	4.9	2.1	5.8	4.8	2.8
Paid leave	8.2	9.5	4.9	8.8	7.2	5.4
Supplemental pay...	7.6................	8.1	8.7	6.9	7.2	9.3
Insurance	9.0	6.9	8.1	8.0	9.7	9.1
Health	8.9	6.9	9.7	7.8	9.6	7.0
Retirement and savings	14	11.2	9.6	14.3	17.	7.0
Legally required[1]	4	3.5	16.	3.9	6	10
	4.3		4		3.3	4

[1] Those benefits which are legally required are OASDI, Medicare, Federal and State unemployment insurance, and workers' compensation.

Table A-3. Differences between workers in nonresidential and residential construction of buildings (NAICS 236),[1] private industry, March data, 2004–09

Item	March 2004	March 2005	March 2006	March 2007	March 2008	March 2009
	Differences in costs per hour worked (*t*-statistics in parentheses)[2]					
Total compensation	$4.22 (1.75)	$4.17 (1.41)	$8.03 (2.52)	$8.96 (3.64)	$12.07 (4.59)	$13.94 (5.04)
Wages and salaries	2.50 (1.51)	3.18 (1.80)	4.62 (2.79)	4.51 (3.43)	6.34 (3.92)	7.82 (4.63)
Total benefits	1.72 (1.72)	.99 (.65)	3.40 (1.99)	4.44 (3.19)	5.73 (4.66)	6.12 (4.54)
Paid leave	.39 (1.81)	.45 (1.80)	.63 (2.17)	.52 (2.35)	.69 (2.87)	.82 (3.20)
Supplemental pay	–.09 (–.24)	–.60 (–.56)	–.13 (–.16)	–.15 (–.16)	.14 (.27)	.06 (.11)
Insurance	.61 (1.61)	.41 (1.11)	1.08 (2.76)	1.55 (4.87)	1.80 (5.07)	1.88 (4.78)
Health	.54 (1.47)	.34 (.96)	.99 (2.72)	1.41 (4.66)	1.65 (4.88)	1.73 (4.62)
Retirement and savings	.59 (1.44)	.70 (1.67)	1.17 (2.45)	1.66 (4.38)	1.96 (4.22)	2.02 (4.02)
Legally required[3]	.21 (.58)	.03 (.09)	.66 (1.90)	.86 (3.61)	1.14 (3.32)	1.35 (4.04)
	Differences in percent of total compensation (*t*-statistics in parentheses)[2]					
Total compensation	–	–	–	–	–	–
Wages and salaries	–2.0 (–1.06)	.8 (.27)	–3.3 (–1.09)	–5.8 (–2.10)	–7.2 (–3.62)	–6.2 (–3.08)
Total benefits	2.0 (1.06)	–.8 (–.27)	3.3 (1.09)	5.8 (2.10)	7.2 (3.62)	6.2 (3.08)
Paid leave	.8 (1.13)	.9 (1.44)	1.0 (1.42)	.5 (1.12)	.7 (1.42)	.7 (1.28)
Supplemental pay	–.8 (–.58)	–2.6 (–.75)	-1.6 (-0.57)	–1.8 (–.59)	–.9 (–.53)	–1.3 (–.76)
Insurance	1.4 (1.23)	.5 (.50)	1.8 (2.24)	3.2 (3.71)	3.4 (3.69)	3.0 (3.13)
Health	1.2 (1.07)	.4 (.33)	1.6 (2.12)	2.8 (3.34)	3.0 (3.39)	2.7 (2.89)
Retirement and savings	1.5 (1.22)	1.8 (1.51)	2.8 (2.24)	4.3 (4.62)	4.7 (4.47)	4.4 (4.10)
Legally required[3]	–.9 (–.74)	–1.5 (–1.18)	–.7 (–1.06)	–.4 (–.64)	–.6 (–.90)	–.5 (–.76)

[1] Each difference is calculated as all or a part of nonresidential workers' compensation minus all or the corresponding part of residential workers' compensation.

[2] Differences are calculated from unrounded averages.

[3] Those benefits which are legally required are OASDI, Medicare, Federal and State unemployment insurance, and workers' compensation.

Table A-4. Differences between nonresidential and residential construction workers in the specialty trade contractors subsector (NAICS 238),[1] private industry, March data, 2004–09

Item	March 2004	March 2005	March 2006	March 2007	March 2008	March 2009
	Differences in costs per hour worked (*t*-statistics in parentheses)[2]					
Total compensation	$8.94	$8.47	$8.28	$7.60	$8.53	$8.78
	(4.80)	(5.88)	(5.92)	(6.42)	(6.35)	(6.42)
Wages and salaries	4.76	4.56	4.19	3.91	4.19	4.17
	(4.83)	(5.21)	(5.36)	(5.78)	(5.59)	(5.32)
Total benefits	4.19	3.91	4.10	3.69	4.34	4.61
	(4.37)	(6.30)	(6.25)	(6.78)	(6.55)	(7.11)
Paid leave	.51	.42	.54	.56	.60	.48
	(4.32)	(3.95)	(5.42)	(4.54)	(5.20)	(3.94)
Supplemental pay	.22	.15	.34	.31	.33	.42
	(1.75)	(1.73)	(3.39)	(3.55)	(3.81)	(3.95)
Insurance	1.32	1.32	1.24	1.27	1.40	1.64
	(3.53)	(6.41)	(5.65)	(7.52)	(6.84)	(7.61)
Health	1.31	1.29	1.18	1.19	1.31	1.55
	(3.57)	(6.45)	(5.58)	(7.39)	(6.92)	(7.56)
Retirement and savings	1.53	1.51	1.32	1.18	1.49	1.60
	(4.82)	(5.16)	(4.08)	(5.91)	(5.07)	(6.80)
Legally required[3]	.60	.50	.65	.37	.51	.47
	(2.35)	(2.43)	(3.41)	(1.96)	(2.62)	(2.68)
	Differences between percent of total compensation (*t*-statistics in parentheses)[2]					
Total compensation	–	–	–	–	–	–
Wages and salaries	–6.3	–5.4	–6.0	–5.4	–6.6	–6.9
	(–3.68)	(–5.35)	(–6.23)	(–6.58)	(–6.48)	(–7.26)
Total benefits	6.3	5.4	6.0	5.4	6.6	6.9
	(3.68)	(5.35)	(6.23)	(6.58)	(6.48)	(7.26)
Paid leave	.9	.6	1.0	1.1	1.1	.6
	(2.32)	(1.48)	(2.54)	(3.03)	(3.39)	(1.97)
Supplemental pay	–.2	–.3	.4	.3	.3	.6
	(–.34)	(–.99)	(1.09)	(1.10)	(.98)	(1.94)
Insurance	3.0	3.0	2.4	2.8	2.9	3.4
	(3.06)	(5.61)	(4.57)	(7.08)	(6.05)	(7.01)
Health	3.0	2.9	2.3	2.6	2.7	3.2
	(3.15)	(5.62)	(4.43)	(6.87)	(6.01)	(6.91)
Retirement and savings	4.4	4.3	3.5	3.2	4.0	4.0
	(5.42)	(5.27)	(3.85)	(5.86)	(5.20)	(6.95)
Legally required[3]	–2.0	–2.2	–1.2	–2.0	–1.7	–1.8
	(–3.34)	(–3.56)	(–2.68)	(–3.80)	(–3.87)	(–5.01)

[1] Each difference is calculated as all or a part of nonresidential workers' compensation minus all or the corresponding part of residential workers' compensation.

[2] Differences are calculated from unrounded averages.

[3] Those benefits which are legally required are OASDI, Medicare, Federal and State unemployment insurance, and workers' compensation.

End Notes

[1] For more on the National Compensation Survey and its products, visit www.bls.gov/ncs (visited Mar. 22, 2010).

[2] For a more thorough description of NAICS, see www.census. gov/eos/www/naics/ (visited Mar. 22, 2010), and for a list of NAICS codes and their titles, see www.census.gov/naics /2007/NAICOD07. HTM#N23 (visited Mar. 22, 2010).

[3] To capture changes in the economy, NAICS codes are revised every 5 years. For construction, a major revision occurred in 2002, but no revisions to the sector were made for 2007. For the tabulations presented in this paper, NAICS codes for construction follow the 2002 and 2007 code structure.

[4] When an establishment is involved in both residential and nonresidential construction projects, BLS assigns the establishment to the type of construction (residential or nonresidential) that generates the most revenue.

[5] For more on the development of the residential and nonresidential construction industries in the specialty trade contractors subsector, see Christopher Manning and John P. Mullins, "Two new construction employment series for specialty trade contractors," *Monthly Labor Review*, October 2006, pp. 14–22, on the Internet at www.bls.gov/opub/ mlr/2006/10/art2full.pdf (visited Mar. 22, 2010).

[6] The numerical data represented in these charts are available from the BLS Web site at www.bls.gov/ces/tables.htm#ee (visited Mar. 22, 2010). Many of these data are revised periodically, and the Web site will reflect the most recent revisions to the data.

[7] The October 2006 edition of the *Monthly Labor Review* featured three articles on employment in the construction industry: John P. Mullins, "Recent employment trends in residential and nonresidential construction," *Monthly Labor Review*, October 2006, pp. 3–13; Manning and Mullins, "Two new construction employment series for specialty trade contractors"; and Matthew Miller, "A visual essay: post-recessionary employment growth related to the housing market," *Monthly Labor Review*, October 2006, pp. 23–34.

[8] SOC is the occupational coding standard for all Federal statistical agencies. See www.bls.gov/ soc (visited Mar. 31, 2010).

[9] Although averages for all residential construction workers and for all nonresidential workers (cross-subsector) are not presented in the tables, they can be calculated by use of the employment counts provided in each column of tables 2 and 3.

[10] The Employment Cost Index and ECEC surveys have only recently been merged into the NCS. In order to reduce the cost of the surveys, both the older Employment Cost Index and ECEC surveys and the current NCS have operated under a rotating sampling design by which approximately 20 percent of private industry establishments are replaced each year. Under this design, several years can pass before published survey results reflect changes that were made to the survey. The adoption of NAICS is one of those survey changes which have taken several years to implement. For more on NCS survey design, see chapter 8 of the *BLS Handbook of Methods* at www.bls.gov/opub/hom/home.htm (visited Mar. 31, 2010).

11 ECEC estimates show the average compensation employers pay workers; because the employment data that go into the calculation are the employment levels at the time of the survey, changes in factors such as distribution of employment among lower and higher paying jobs from one survey period to the next can affect average compensation figures even if the pay scales of the sampled occupations have not changed.

[12] See *Employment Cost Index—Supplemental Data: Health insurance, private industry, 12-month percent change in employer costs per hour worked* (Bureau of Labor Statistics, Jan. 29, 2010), on the Internet at www.bls.gov/ncs/ect/sp/echealth.pdf (visited Mar. 31, 2010).

[13] The NCS program publishes estimates on the percent of employees required to share in the costs of medical plan premiums and on employees' average contributions (in dollars). For more on these benefit statistics, see www.bls.gov/ncs/ncspubs.htm (visited Mar. 31, 2010). The NCS program has not tabulated estimates for the detailed construction industries examined in this paper, however.

[14] Caution should be exercised when interpreting cost levels for individual benefits such as retirement and savings, because the relative standard errors are high. Relative standard error (RSE) is the sampling error of an estimate as a percent of that estimate. For most ECEC published series of benefit costs, RSEs range from 1 percent to 50 percent. The RSEs of the retirement and savings estimates for the industries in this study range from 17.8 percent to 35.5 percent. Typically, an RSE is inversely related to the size of the sample in question.

[15] These cost differences are calculated with unrounded industry averages. See tables A-3 and A-4 of the appendix for cost differences.

[16] Occupational mix was modeled by assigning an indicator variable to each of the six-digit SOC occupations present in the microdata. Geographical area and occupational characteristic variables were modeled in a similar way—by constructing indicator variables for each. Establishment size was modeled as the logarithm of reported establishment employment. The variable of interest, industry, also was modeled as an indicator variable.

[17] Each occupation that is selected during the NCS collection process is evaluated and slotted into 1 of 15 "work levels," which follow the federal government's General Schedule. For NCS purposes, multiple levels of the same occupation—accountants, for example—are considered as separate occupations. This occupational l an establishment using the same criteria throughout. For information on the NCS occupational leveling process, see www.bls.gov/ncs/ocs/sp/ncbr0004.pdf (visited Apr. 5, 2010.) With the merger of the ECI/ ECEC sample into the broader NCS wage sample, occupational leveling information is now collected for all sampled occupations. Leveling information show—among other characteristics—the knowledge and skill levels of workers within particular occupations. Leveling information may prove important for understanding differences between residential and nonresidential construction. Work continues in this area, and for this reason a complete analysis of the regression model is not presented in this article.

[18] Level of skill and other characteristics, however, are not controlled for when an occupation's wage in one industry is compared with its wage in another industry, and, consequently, these characteristics can influence the difference in average wage that is calculated.

[19] The two major occupational groups reporting higher earnings for residential construction workers were life, physical, and social science occupations, and building and grounds cleaning and maintenance occupations. The former accounted for less one-tenth of one percent of employment in residential construction, and the latter accounted for about 1 percent of employment in residential construction.

[20] For other occupational wage and employment data on the construction of buildings subsector for May 2008, visit www.bls.gov/ oes/2008/may/naics3_236000.htm (visited Mar. 31, 2010).

[21] See ftp://ftp.bls.gov/pub/special.requests/ocwc/ect/ecec-eveling process allows one to rank and compare all occupations that are randomly selected in qrtn.pdf (visited Mar. 31, 2010) for ECEC tables by worker characteristics from March 2004 to December 2009.

[22] For estimates of the median weekly earnings of union workers by occupation or industry, see data from BLS's Current Population Survey, many of which are available at www.bls.gov/cps/lfcharacteristics. htm#union (visited Mar. 31, 2010).

[23] Standard errors for the data on union membership and establishment size in this article are not available, and, consequently, comparisons across periods should be done with caution.

[24] The effect of unionization on pay levels is not universally causal: issues of endogeneity must be considered. The impact of unionization may be more an indirect correlation than a direct one, as in incidences in which unions effect better trained and safer groups of workers whose pay reflects the training. See David Card, "The effect of unions on the structure of wages: a longitudinal analysis," *Econometrica*, July 1996, pp. 957–79.

[25] The assignment of union status can differ between the NCS and the Current Population Survey (CPS). In the CPS, unionization refers to members of a labor union or an employee association similar to a union. See www.bls.gov/news.release/union2.nr0.htm (visited Mar. 31, 2010). The NCS definition of union status is similar to that of the CPS, but it stipulates that the union be recognized as a bargaining agent for all workers in any occupation that is selected for the sample and that there also be a signed mutually binding collective bargaining agreement that includes at least earnings provisions.

INDEX

J

L

M

N

O

P

R

S

T

U

V

W